The START-OPS PLAY BOOK

OPERATIONALIZE YOUR CONSUMER PRODUCT VENTURE

DAVID DiLORETO

Published by Start-Ops Playbook, LLC

Printed in the United States of America

Start-Ops Playbook, LLC
The Start-Ops Playbook: Operationalize your consumer product venture

ISBN 979-8-9936915-0-3

First Edition

Table of
CONTENTS

Introduction vii

PILLAR 1: FORECASTING AND PLANNING 1

1-A. The Situation: Setting the Scene 1

1-B. The Core: Section Contents. 2

BILL OF MATERIALS. 3

ENTERPRISE RESOURCE PLANNING (ERP) 4

DEMAND PLAN 7

SUPPLY PLAN. 12

MATERIAL RESOURCE PLAN (MRP) 19

FINANCIAL STATEMENT MODELS. 24

1-C. The Wrap: Quick Facts for Benchmarks 29

PILLAR 2: PROCUREMENT. 31

2-A. The Situation: Setting the Scene 31

2-B. The Core: Section Contents. 32

CATALOG OF SUPPLIERS 32

NEGOTIATION STRATEGY 34

NEGOTIABLE POINTS. 35

RFP (REQUEST FOR PROPOSAL). 37

CONTRACTS. 40

2-C. The Wrap: Quick Facts for Benchmarks 43

PILLAR 3: QUALITY 47
3-A. The Situation: Setting the Scene 47
3-B. The Core: Section Contents 48
OPERATING PROCEDURES AND TESTING 48
COMPLIANCE DOCUMENTATION 52
MANUFACTURING STANDARDS 56
3-C. The Wrap: Quick Facts for Benchmarks 58

PILLAR 4: MANUFACTURING 61
4-A. The Situation: Setting the Scene 61
4-B. The Core: Section Contents 62
IDENTIFYING AND VETTING A CO-PACKER 63
PILOT PRODUCTION 70
MANUFACTURING AGREEMENT 72
INVENTORY MANAGEMENT 77
SYSTEMS AND COMMUNCATION 82
CHAMPION/CHALLENGER MODEL 83
RELATIONSHIP SUSTAINABILTY 84
4-C. The Wrap: Quick Facts for Benchmarks 86

PILLAR 5: DISTRIBUTION 89
5-A. The Situation: Setting the Scene 89
5-B. The Core: Section Contents 90
3PL REQUIREMENTS 90
NETWORK DESIGN 92
WHOLESALE NORMS 97
ECOMMERCE NORMS 102
ORDER MANAGEMENT 106
5-C. The Wrap: Quick Facts for Benchmarks 108

PILLAR 6: NEW PRODUCT DEVELOPMENT 113

6-A. The Situation: Setting the Scene 113

6-B. The Core: Section Contents. 115

INNOVATION BASICS 115

PORTFOLIO ASSESSMENT 117

STANDARD TIMELINES 120

INTRODUCING THE NEW PRODUCTS 122

TESTING AND VALIDATION 124

6-C. The Wrap: Quick Facts for Benchmarks 126

In Closing 127

Appendix A: Acronyms & Abbreviations. 131

About the Author 135

Website and Social Media 136

INTRODUCTION

It was March 2020, and I was facing a truly frightening proposition: how the hell do you build an operating model for a non-alcoholic booze company when nothing like this exists? This was my situation when I took the reins, directing the operations at Ritual Zero Proof in our first year of business.

On day one, our CEO David Crooch said something that had a profound impact on me: "there's no playbook for running Ops at a startup company. We're going to need you to figure it out." I spent the next several years piecing together the components of a successful supply chain. As it started coming together, I thought back to David's comment about the absence of an official playbook. My conclusion: there really should be one. The following playbook is a synthesis of my experience building a startup's operations in a burgeoning yet nascent category in consumer goods.

The focal point of this playbook is consumer package goods. I expect it will be applicable to any product-based company and could even provide some insights for a tech startup. In behavioral science, they call this concept "knowledge transfer" (taking the lessons from one application and applying them to another). Apparently, most people suck at this practice, but we Ops folks are a different breed. We need to learn hard lessons in one place and apply them in another arena. Hence, the origin of this playbook. As a starting point, we'll assume that you already have the first product developed and financing in place. The scope of this book answers the proverbial question facing all startups: "Now what?"

In terms of the format, this is going to be a hybrid of a narrative account with practical lessons. We're going to go light on the fluff and deep in the rough. Although intentionally short in total length, I recommend reading only one section per sitting. After you finish the section, it's crucial that you attempt to apply the lessons to your company's data. At Ritual, we used to say, "we're building the car as we drive it." This may not sound like a logical approach, but it's actually the best way to learn at a startup. Another common theme throughout the playbook is the importance of trade-offs. The team often heard me recite the mantra, "It's not a perfect plan, but it's the best plan available". It usually got a few laughs, and you have to stick with the classics, but I really do mean it. A fatal mistake in startups (and life, for that matter) is making perfect the enemy of the good. Finally, my primary objective was to write something that I could say, "If only I had this info when I was 34, I'd have made far fewer mistakes." My hope is this book will prevent you from making the mistakes in the first place.

Lastly, some of these exercises are a bit challenging to explain verbally. For this reason, I added supplemental spreadsheets, with comments on how I built these models. Find these on the website at startopsplaybook.com/resources. Be sure to access these materials and work through the sections with your actual numbers. Also, I started a YouTube channel called ***The Start-Ops Playbook (@start_ops_playbook)***. There, you'll find demos on some of the more technical aspects, so be sure to check it out. Now let's dive in and start building while we drive.

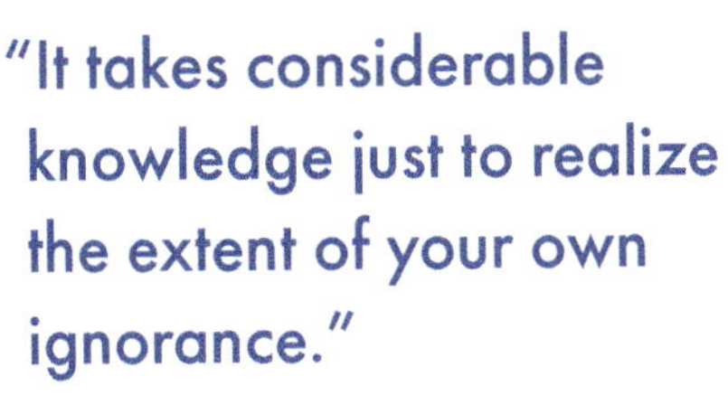

"It takes considerable knowledge just to realize the extent of your own ignorance."

– Thomas Sowell

PILLAR 1

FORECASTING AND PLANNING

1-A. The Situation: Setting the Scene

I often hear aspiring entrepreneurs say: "I have some great ideas, but I don't know how to get started." When building a startup's operating model, forecasting and planning are the place to start. Another flashback to week one at Ritual: sales had begun on eCommerce a few months earlier and we were rapidly approaching shipment of our first big order to Total Wine & More. Production was desperately needed, and I was responsible for figuring that out.

The team sent over all the planning files we had in place, which was basically a single PDF document with the product formulations. That was it. The task was clear: determine the number of bottles to produce, buy the materials, get them in-house, and get the product made. It was a true blank slate to build the tools needed, which is the type of project that should be both liberating and daunting to any real Start-Ops leader.

Over the next few months, I began to cultivate the baseline tools required to conduct accurate forecasting and planning. These tools provide the foundation for the most basic steps in getting your startup off the ground. The statistics show that about 50% of startups fail to survive the first five years and 90% fail in the long-run. Inaccurate forecasting is a sure-fire way to ensure your company joins that party. Forecast too much product, and you run out of cash. Forecast too little, and you run out of inventory, lose sales, and eventually run out of cash.

This is an area where the Ops team differs from the other functional departments. In most cases, with sales and marketing, there are minimums or maximums. For sales, it's monthly case targets and for marketing, it's something like minimum impressions or conversion rate. There's a number to hit and once you reach the target, anything more (or less) is gravy. Not in operations. Operations is much more akin to economics. There's an optimal price where supply and demand meet. Likewise, there's an optimal number of days-on-hand inventory.

In this section, the first plank in the Start-Ops playbook, we'll discuss how to go from a single formula sheet to a robust planning system, with a focus on optimizing inventory, maximizing case-fill-rate, and ensuring sufficient cash-on-hand.

1-B. The Core: Section Contents

- Objective: How to build from a PDF formula sheet to a series of flexible, integrated models
- Key Components:
    - Bill of Materials
    - Enterprise Resource Planning (ERP)
    - Demand Plan
    - Supply Plan
    - Material Resource Plan (MRP)

BILL OF MATERIALS

The bill of materials (BOM) is, quite simply, a derivation of the formula sheet into a workable format. The output of your product development exercise (which precedes the Start-Ops playbook) will be a finished formula sheet similar to Figure 1 below. This sheet serves as the instructions for creating one batch of your product in bulk. If it's a beverage product, that batch could be anywhere from 500 to 10,000 gallons.

Formula House

PlaceboPump 1.0 - 1,000 gal batch
Fruit Punch
16 fl oz
#100010

Lookup	Ingredient	Batch Qty		16 fl oz Qty	
		qty	units	qty	units
RM_Erythritol	Erythritol	120	lbs.	0.01500	lbs.
RM_Citric Acid	Citric Acid	10	lbs.	0.00125	lbs.
RM_Vitamin and Plant Extract	Vitamin and Plant Extract	11	gal	0.00138	gal
RM_Fruit Punch Flavor	Fruit Punch Flavor	21	gal	0.00263	gal
RM_Sodium Benzoate	Sodium Benzoate	2	lbs.	0.00025	lbs.
RM_Water	Water	960	gal	0.12000	gal

Figure 1. Formula Sheet

The BOM translates this bulk formulation from a full batch down to unit-level terms. We want to know how much material is needed to make one bottle, one packet, one pouch, or whatever it is your company produces. The output will look like Figure 2 below. The BOM's purpose is to provide the bottoms-up data at the unit level for later planning exercises. Formulation works in batches from the top-down; supply planning and material planning works in total number of sales units from the bottom-up.

For example, when a contract manufacturer plans to run production, they plan that production around batch size, which is typically based on the size of the vessel (i.e. how big the mixing tank is). If they have a 2K gallon tank, they will require their clients to provide batches in ~1K gallon increments. As a result, they'll batch up 1K gallons or 2K gallons and fill as many units as they can until the tank is empty. However, the brand team plans at the consumer and/or retailer level. We'll cover this in detail during the demand plan section, but essentially, your team will forecast how many bottles or bars or capsules you think can be sold over the next 3, 6, or 12 months. Then you need to plan the appropriate materials (MRP–material resource plan) and total number of units (supply plan). Efficiently completing this exercise requires a tool to translate batches to units; enter the BOM.

You'll probably notice I was bouncing around a lot in the above section. Get used to it! If you want a role with a perfectly linear progression from point A to B to C, get a job at the Federal Reserve (this comes with the added bonus of zero accountability). A Start-Ops leader must be able to swiftly pivot from bottom up to top down, pre-process to post-process, and product development to commercialization.

ENTERPRISE RESOURCE PLANNING (ERP)

Once the BOM is in place, it is crucial to get an ERP system off the ground. Typically, people think of SAP or Oracle NetSuite when they think of an ERP, but many "lite" web-based versions exist. Get yourself a web-based ERP designed for smaller organizations. I used

Bill of Materials

SKU	COGS/Btl
FP_Wholesale	$1.52
FP_eCommerce	$1.62

Product	Channel	Var Name	Ingredient/Packaging	Cost/Sale U	Qty/Sale U	Qty/Bot	Cost/Bot
Fruit Punch	Wholesale	FP_Wholesale	RM_Erythritol	$75.00	50	0.0150	$0.0225
Fruit Punch	Wholesale	FP_Wholesale	RM_Citric Acid	$100.00	50	0.0013	$0.0025
Fruit Punch	Wholesale	FP_Wholesale	RM_Vitamin and Plant Extrac	$6,325.00	55	0.0014	$0.1581
Fruit Punch	Wholesale	FP_Wholesale	RM_Fruit Punch Flavor	$17,050.00	55	0.0026	$0.8138
Fruit Punch	Wholesale	FP_Wholesale	RM_Sodium Benzoate	$175.00	50	0.0003	$0.0009
Fruit Punch	Wholesale	FP_Wholesale	PKG_16z Bottle	$0.22	1	1.0000	$0.2200
Fruit Punch	Wholesale	FP_Wholesale	PKG_Cap	$0.15	1	1.0000	$0.1500
Fruit Punch	Wholesale	FP_Wholesale	PKG_Label	$0.08	1	1.0000	$0.0800
Fruit Punch	Wholesale	FP_Wholesale	PKG_12pk Case	$0.85	1	0.0833	$0.0708
Fruit Punch	eCommerce	FP_eCommerce	RM_Erythritol	$75.00	50	0.0150	$0.0225
Fruit Punch	eCommerce	FP_eCommerce	RM_Citric Acid	$100.00	50	0.0013	$0.0025
Fruit Punch	eCommerce	FP_eCommerce	RM_Vitamin and Plant Extrac	$6,325.00	55	0.0014	$0.1581
Fruit Punch	eCommerce	FP_eCommerce	RM_Fruit Punch Flavor	$17,050.00	55	0.0026	$0.8138
Fruit Punch	eCommerce	FP_eCommerce	RM_Sodium Benzoate	$175.00	50	0.0003	$0.0009
Fruit Punch	eCommerce	FP_eCommerce	PKG_16z Bottle	$0.22	1	1.0000	$0.2200
Fruit Punch	eCommerce	FP_eCommerce	PKG_Cap	$0.15	1	1.0000	$0.1500
Fruit Punch	eCommerce	FP_eCommerce	PKG_Label	$0.08	1	1.0000	$0.0800
Fruit Punch	eCommerce	FP_eCommerce	PKG_6pk_eComm Case	$1.05	1	0.1667	$0.1750

Figure 2. Bill of Materials

Core (https://www.cin7.com/) and it was perfectly adequate for our first five years of operations.

ERP Components

The ERP will be used to conduct four fundamental business processes:

1. ***Purchase Orders (POs):*** orders your company sends out to purchase raw and packaging materials
2. ***Sales Orders (SOs):*** orders of finished goods shipped out to your customers
3. ***Material Assemblies:*** conversion of raw and packaging materials into finished goods
4. ***Inventory Management:*** maintaining, analyzing, adjusting inventory levels of finished goods, raw, and packaging materials

These processes are needed to manage all your internal forecasting and accounting. POs enable you to receive and maintain inventory of materials. Sales orders confirm how many units were sold and record revenue. Assemblies enable the conversion of bottles, caps, etc. into finished products, meaning those materials are no longer available for future production. The inventory management section provides the final summary of all these steps with a current inventory level.

Technically, all the above could be done by managing a series of independent spreadsheets. I've heard of several companies that delayed implementing an ERP and managed all this activity through spreadsheets for as long as two years. **It's hard to overstate just how stupid this approach is.** These systems are not that expensive, going for as low as $2-5K per year. If you're not prepared to spend $3K a year on an ERP system, you're not ready to outlay $20-100K on a production run, which is probably someone else's cash. You can't make bricks without clay, and you can't run this playbook without clean data. A solid ERP system with some basic operating hygiene is the best way to ensure reliable inputs in your models.

DEMAND PLAN

Now that we have some nuts and bolts in place, it's time to finally use our brains. Few tools exist in a business plan that impact more aspects of your company, simultaneously, than the demand plan. Consequently, it's really important that you don't screw this up. The demand plan is a forecast of customer sales for the next 12, 24, and 36 months.

The demand plan is the baseline sales forecast. You need this tool for your entire business to function properly. It tells you how much cash to raise, how many people to hire, how to set targets for your sales and marketing teams, and most importantly for the ops team, how much product to make and hold. Hopefully this is about as clear as how to fasten your seatbelt on an airplane.

There are a few different methodologies, so which one you use will be highly dependent on the state of your business. If you have an early-stage business with few customers, you may prefer the simplicity of the top-down method. If further along with a stable of consistent customers, you will likely prefer the accuracy of the bottom-up method.

Top-Down Method

This is how we started at Ritual. You calculate an aspirational yet achievable annual target and work backwards to monthly totals, based on projected seasonality. The best way to do this is to benchmark against other comparable brands. Acquiring these data can be fairly difficult. If you have an investor group or strategic partner, they can be a great resource. A less preferable but workable option is to apply capital constraints (i.e. take your budget for the year, figure out the capacity to produce, market, and sell, and go from there). It's important to recognize that this method is what we call SWAGU. It's rough, unsophisticated, and usually a tweak or two away from complete nonsense. But, you have to start somewhere so take a look at Figure 3 below for an example. After the first year, it gets a whole lot easier when you can analyze real data.

Item	Total	Units	Notes
Total Addressable Market	$50,000.00	($ '000)	small category
Market share	1%		assumes you capture 1% in year one (nascent category)
Revenue year one	$500.00	($ '000)	
Blended cost per bottle	$1.38		assumes product mix of 50% fruit punch, 40% grape, 10% pimento punch
Price per bottle	$3.06		55% gross margin ex logisitics
Price per case	$36.76		12 pack case
Cases sold	13,601		Revenue / (Price/Case)
Volume forecast	**14,000**		

Figure 3. Top Down SWAGU Forecast

Bottom-Up Method

This is a much more professional approach, and you should move to this as quickly as it can accurately be achieved. At ***Kraft-Heinz***, we used a triangulation method, which can be adopted fairly early in your business lifecycle. We started using this method in Q4 of our first year with an acceptable level of accuracy (+/- 20% of actuals).

The triangulation is compiled with these three legs on the stool:

1. ***Historical Data – Finance Team:*** The finance lead (possibly you in an early-stage startup), will need to compile historical sales to calculate typical volumes and sales velocity (rate of sale – ROS). The aggregation of these data will build a baseline for expected sales.
2. ***New Sales Inputs – Sales Team:*** The sales team should supplement the baseline forecast with any recent news (good or bad) that will impact the sales forecast. For an early-stage company, this often takes the form of a new customer authorization, with the load in quantity and date. On the flip side, it's possible that you pissed off a customer and they need to be removed from your baseline forecast.
3. ***New Marketing Plans – Marketing Team:*** Lastly, the marketing team should input any upcoming activations and the projected lift. This exercise is much simpler in ecommerce, where clear trends will surface on marketing effectiveness for paid media spend (i.e. ROAS — return on ad spend for Amazon). If the team is conducting a digital activation like a video on YouTube or Meta, it's going to be more difficult, but you'll need to include some estimates based on historical campaigns or competitive benchmarks.

A natural tension will emerge between the Finance and Ops teams during this exercise. For Finance, a "conservative" approach means erring on the side of underestimating sales. This ensures you won't run out of cash. However, for the Ops team, conservatism requires precisely the opposite approach. You'll want to ensure sufficient inventory coverage, which we'll cover in the next section on supply planning. In the end, this scenario is a bit like baseball, where the tie goes to the runner; Finance is the runner. It's important that Finance doesn't significantly overestimate sales projections, as this can also create serious financial issues, including cash shortages and disappointed investors. Part of being a great supply planner is ensuring coverage of the demand plan with a buffer; how much buffer depends on several key variables, which we'll discuss next.

The bottoms-up forecast uses the following formula:

Total Demand (cases per month) = # of Doors × # of SKUs per Door × Rate of Sale

- ***# of Doors:*** Total number of stores that carry your product
- ***# of SKUs per Door:*** Average number of your total SKUs the retailer carries. So, imagine you have 3 total SKUs. Then assume you are in 200 doors with a retailer. Lastly, assume you have 3 SKUs in 100 of those doors and 2 SKUs in the remaining 100 doors. The average # of SKUs is 2.5
- ***Rate of Sale:*** Average number of cases sold per door per time period (in this case, I use months, but it could also be tracked in weeks)

See the ***Demand Forecast*** section of the supplemental materials for the detailed example and Figure 4 below.

In summary, I calculated two different totals with the two different methodologies: 14,000 cases with the SWAGU method and ~16,000 cases with bottom-up build. The major weakness with the SWAGU method is the need to project your market share, which is very difficult to forecast in year one. To set a realistic number, examine similar

12 pack case sales per month														
Type	Retailer	Jan-26	Feb-26	Mar-26	Apr-26	May-26	Jun-26	Jul-26	Aug-26	Sep-26	Oct-26	Nov-26	Dec-26	Total
National	Kroger	200	200	200	200	200	200	200	200	200	200	200	200	2,400
National	Target	0	0	0	0	0	0	0	0	0	100	100	100	300
National	Wal-Mart	120	120	120	120	120	120	120	120	120	120	120	120	1,440
National	7-Eleven	600	600	600	600	600	800	800	800	600	600	600	600	7,800
Regional	Aldi	75	75	75	75	75	75	125	125	125	125	125	125	1,200
Regional	Shop-rite	84	84	84	84	84	84	84	84	84	84	84	84	1,008
Regional	Stop-n-Shop	150	150	150	150	150	150	150	150	150	150	150	150	1,800
Local	Bill's Grocery	0	0	0	0	0	0	0	0	0	0	0	0	3
Local	Ahmed's Grocery	0	0	0	0	0	0	0	0	0	0	0	0	4
Local	Nora's Grocery	2	2	2	2	2	2	2	2	2	2	2	2	18
Total		**1,231**	**1,231**	**1,231**	**1,231**	**1,231**	**1,431**	**1,481**	**1,481**	**1,281**	**1,381**	**1,381**	**1,381**	**15,973**

Figure 4. Bottom-Up Forecast

product entries in similar categories. To reiterate, shift to bottom-up forecast as soon as you have confidence in the 3 pieces of data mentioned above: **# of Doors, # of SKUs per Door, and Rate of Sale**.

SUPPLY PLAN

Think of the demand plan like a Hinge profile. Get it in place, looking shiny with your exotic photos from SE Asia, several pithy quips, and your impressive educational background. Now it's time to actually go on the date. The demand plan is a forecast, whereas the supply plan sets in motion all the downstream action that elevates your product from ***"a thought to something bought."*** The supply plan is a SKU-by-SKU breakdown of the production needed for the next 12, 24, and 36 months.

The Supply plan is the primary input to direct 4 crucial outputs:

1. Inform the MRP (material resource plan) on raw and packaging material needs (quantities and delivery dates prior to production)
2. Secure line time with the contract manufacturer and execute the production runs
3. Determine storage levels of on-hand inventory to support order fulfillment across future growth plans
4. Calculate cash needs in the cash flow forecast, which informs capital raise totals

The Ending Inventory Method

The methodology for supply planning is universal and relies on this thing we call math. I've encountered some folks in the past who couldn't conceptually grasp this formula in practice. I've learned that not everyone has an Ops-based mentality and no matter what you do, you won't get the key concepts to hit home. Keep this in mind in your hiring, and I highly recommend assigning a 1-2 hour project using Excel and some basic inventory movements to validate this skill in new hires. The basic formulas for supply planning are:

$$\textit{Ending Inventory} = \textit{Beginning Inventory} - \textit{Projected Sales} + \textit{Production}$$

$$\textit{Rate of Sale (ROS)} = \frac{\textit{Projected Sales over a period of time (i.e. 3 months of sales)}}{\textit{Period of time (i.e. ~89 – 92 days)}} = \textit{Sales/day}$$

$$\textit{Days on Hand Inventory (DOH)} = \frac{\textit{Ending Inventory}}{\textit{ROS}} = \textit{x days of inventory}$$

It looks a little complicated but it's actually quite simple (see the ***Supply plan summary*** in the supplemental materials). Take your starting inventory, layer in your demand plan for projected sales, and create a new line for production. Run the formula and determine ending inventory. That's one month. Then, extend this formula over the next 12 months. The adjustable here is ***production quantity per month***. Keep adjusting it until it reaches your target DOH number, which means ***days on hand***.

You calculate DOH using the ending inventory and rate of sale (ROS). ROS is determined by selecting a logical time period and calculating average sales per day. I like to use a 3-month rolling period. Meaning, if analyzing in June, take the projected sales from July-September and divide it by the total number of days for that period (92 days). Once you have ROS, take your ending inventory level and divide it by ROS to get the total days of inventory on hand at the end of the month. Initially, you should build out a basic Excel model (see Figure 5).

Factor	DOH (Days on Hand)
Absolute Min	50
Target Min	70
Target Max	90
Absolute Max	110

Days per month	31	28	31	30
Fruit Punch	**Jan-26**	**Feb-26**	**Mar-26**	**Apr-26**
1. Inventory	1,500	2,075	1,451	1,826
2. Forecast Demand	625	625	625	625
3. Open PO (Prod Order)	1,200	0	1,000	0
4. Ending Inv	2,075	1,451	1,826	1,201
5. Days On-Hand	99	71	84	53
Grape	**Jan-26**	**Feb-26**	**Mar-26**	**Apr-26**
1. Inventory	900	1,400	900	1,401
2. Forecast Demand	500	500	500	500
3. Open PO (Prod Order)	1,000	0	1,000	0
4. Ending Inv	1,400	900	1,401	901
5. Days On-Hand	83	55	81	49
Pimento Punch	**Jan-26**	**Feb-26**	**Mar-26**	**Apr-26**
1. Inventory	400	425	300	395
2. Forecast Demand	125	125	125	125
3. Open PO (Prod Order)	150	0	220	0
4. Ending Inv	425	300	395	270
5. Days On-Hand	101	74	91	59

In this model, I adjusted Column 3 (highlighted in pink), called ***Open PO (production order)***. I used conditional formatting to identify my target DOH range (70-90 days), along with moderate and out of range criteria. For example, look at the Fruit Punch section at the top. You can see DOH falls to 53 days at the end of April. Based on my targets, anything less than 50 is in the danger zone, meaning I risk out-of-stocks if a large order is received. This is why I increased

Adjustable cell	Target range
Calculated cell	Moderate range
	Out of range

31	30	31	31	30	31	30	31
May-26	Jun-26	Jul-26	Aug-26	Sep-26	Oct-26	Nov-26	Dec-26
1,201	1,876	1,152	1,902	1,152	1,802	1,103	1,803
625	725	750	750	650	700	700	700
1,300	0	1,500	0	1,300	0	1,400	0
1,876	1,152	1,902	1,152	1,802	1,103	1,803	1,103
78	49	83	51	79	48	77	47
May-26	Jun-26	Jul-26	Aug-26	Sep-26	Oct-26	Nov-26	Dec-26
901	1,601	1,021	1,521	922	1,502	942	1,682
500	580	600	600	520	560	560	560
1,200	0	1,100	0	1,100	0	1,300	0
1,601	1,021	1,521	922	1,502	942	1,682	1,122
83	55	83	51	82	54	97	67
May-26	Jun-26	Jul-26	Aug-26	Sep-26	Oct-26	Nov-26	Dec-26
270	395	250	375	225	395	256	366
125	145	150	150	130	140	140	140
250	0	275	0	300	0	250	0
395	250	375	225	395	256	366	226
82	54	82	50	87	57	82	52

Figure 5. Basic Excel Supply Plan

May production to 1,300 cases (higher than previous months). This balances out nicely for the rest of the year, hovering at an average DOH of 68 from May-December (around the low end of target). You should do this exercise every month on a regular cadence (i.e. the first week of every month).

To complete the Supply Plan, we must have a target DOH. Target DOH depends on several variables:

Target DOH Factors

1. *Industry Benchmarks:* Determine the closest comp to your industry/category and use this as a starting point.
2. *Stage of Company:* The earlier the stage, the less data and the less reliable the demand plan. This creates a need for more inventory than benchmarks suggest.
3. *Category Volatility*: Nascent, growing categories are much more difficult to predict and often don't have full seasonality curves built. This also creates a need for more inventory than the typical benchmarks suggest.
4. *Cash Constraints:* Depending on your financing plan, you might have constraints on the quantity of product you can reasonably expect to hold (i.e. you can't tie up all your money in inventory or you won't have the marketing dollars available to sell it through).
5. *Route to Market:* Your geographic expansion plan will be crucial. It follows the same pattern as above. Less markets = easier to forecast, more markets = harder to forecast, requiring more inventory. This one is particularly important because geographic expansion is often based on customer acceptance (i.e. you obtain authorization with Kroger, it is contingent upon ability to support 20 states). This can result in an all-or-nothing scenario, whereby failure to support the entire PO means you lose the customer entirely.
6. *Product and Material Lead Time:* Shorter lead times = less inventory needed, longer lead times = more inventory needed. It also helps to have two contract manufacturers (discussed later), as this unlocks additional capacity. The

input materials (lead time on bottles, caps, raw materials) and contract manufacturer flexibility determine the lead times.

After you determine the target DOH, you can implement your supply planning process. I recommend keeping the DOH slightly higher in the beginning, then ratcheting it down as you gain more confidence in your demand plan. If you can add a backup contract manufacturer, that will enable you to reduce DOH, as it provides another lever to quickly build inventory in a pinch (more to come in part 4). This DOH will need to be extended throughout your entire distribution network. I'll expand on this at the warehouse level in the distribution section.

Once you progress to a later stage and enhance some of your IT resources, you can build this out in a data visualization tool like Power BI (see Figure 6—ignore the numbers as that model is purely for illustrative purposes). Later, there are tools like ***Blue Yonder***, that automate a lot of these processes. This will vary significantly, but I would gauge it at the revenue level.

- $0-10M: Use excel
- $10-50M: Build a custom dashboard
- >$50M: Use integrated tool (i.e. Blue Yonder, SAP, Net-suite, etc.)

Power BI is a fantastic tool that I use every day. However, depending on your background, don't sink too much time into building models. If you don't have experience with programming, they can be pretty finicky to get off the ground and require some coding knowledge (DAX). I wasted a bunch of time in the early stages trying to learn how to build the models and create the dashboards. This is time I should

Year	2025					2026					
Item	AUG	SEP	OCT	NOV	DEC	JAN	FEB	MAR	APR	MAY	JUN
16oz Fruit Punch											
Inventory	68166	61827	98641	75715	109982	71445	56441	81667	47780	61256	71326
Forecast Demand	6339	23187	22926	25733	38537	55003	34773	33886	36525	39930	41533
Open PO (Prod Order)	0	60000	0	60000	0	40000	60000	0	50000	50000	50000
Ending Inv	61827	98641	75715	109982	71445	56441	81667	47780	61256	71326	79792
Days On-Hand	82	108	65	87	53	43	68	38	47	53	58
16oz Grape											
Inventory	56893	52759	87638	72687	105904	80772	94899	72220	110122	86302	120260
Forecast Demand	4134	15122	14951	16781	25133	35872	22679	22099	23820	26041	27088
Open PO (Prod Order)	0	50000	0	50000	0	50000	0	60000	0	60000	0
Ending Inv	52759	87638	72687	105904	80772	94899	72220	110122	86302	120260	93172
Days On-Hand	107	148	95	128	93	110	93	135	102	137	104
16oz Pimento Punch											
Inventory	70448	64799	104133	83698	140762	106413	117388	116394	116191	123636	118046
Forecast Demand	5649	20667	20434	22936	34349	49025	30994	30203	32554	35589	37019
Open PO (Prod Order)	0	60000	0	80000	0	60000	30000	30000	40000	30000	40000
Ending Inv	64799	104133	83698	140762	106413	117388	116394	116191	123636	118046	121027
Days On-Hand	96	128	80	124	89	100	109	104	107	99	99

Figure 6. Power BI Supply Plan Tool

have spent writing quality SOPs, sourcing alternate material vendors, and commissioning a second co-packer (all covered later). Instead, I was watching YouTube videos that typically weren't specific enough to overcome the challenge I was facing.

A general startup rule of thumb: if you can't make much progress after a week locked away in a conference room, hire someone to do it! Your time will be better served by hiring someone off Upwork and focusing on mission-critical objectives.

MATERIAL RESOURCE PLAN (MRP)

We've made it to the final operational input. Unfortunately, this is likely the most time-consuming and tedious element of a startup operator's responsibilities. In fact, it was one of the activities I hated the most, eclipsed only by inventory management (to be discussed later). What this task lacks in intellectual stimulation, it compensates for in consequence; it can make or break your early-stage production runs.

The MRP is the combination of the BOM and the supply plan. It is a bottom-up build of raw and packaging material quantities and delivery dates, prior to the production run. The MRP is required to plan and procure your production run materials. It tells you how much citric acid, flavor ingredients, bottles, corks, pouches, boxes, etc. to order and when these materials need to be in-house to complete production. **A mistake in one component on the MRP can result in a missed production run,** leading to out of stocks, missed sales, and eventually running out of cash.

When I first started at Ritual, there was an issue involving a kg to lbs conversion that created a shortage of one raw material. We couldn't run production until this discrepancy was resolved, and it was serious challenge to get more material on such short notice. These are the kinds of issues that can blow up a company as fast as a space shuttle. Therefore, it's paramount to have a reliable MRP model in place and a very diligent operator overseeing the process.

The Ending Inventory Method Remix

Daunting as that may sound, there is good news: you already know how to build it. That is, assuming you learned how to complete the supply plan. The MRP follows the same pattern as the supply plan, with a couple notable additions:

1. Take the supply plan finished good totals and build it into a tab on the model (i.e. we need to produce 1,000 bottles of Fruit Punch in March of this year).
2. Add a tab for the BOM, which builds up all the individual components of one unit (i.e. we need 1,000 bottles, 1,000 corks, x grams of citric acid, y gallons of flavor, etc.).
3. Create a tab that lists out all these individual components and calculates the amount needed to produce the total.
4. Add a 10-20% buffer on materials to account for shrinkage/waste.
5. Determine lead times for each item and work backwards to calculate order dates; **plan on a material delivery date of 4–8 weeks prior to the production run.**

A completed MRP should look like Figure 7 below. As with the supply plan, you'll follow the progression from Excel to visualization tool to automated software. This is a good time to reference the formulas in the ***MRP summary*** section of the supplemental materials.

Major items to highlight here include the SKU mix and units. You will have 3 types of items to order:

1. ***Generic Items:*** Uniform materials across all SKUs, such as glass bottles. You will likely start with 1 uniform bottle for the full portfolio of products. These are the easiest to forecast. Take the total demand for finished products and that's how many bottles are needed.
2. ***SKU-Specific Eaches:*** Items that require 1 unit for each finished product of a specific SKU, like a Fruit Punch label. You will need 1 label for each bottle of Fruit Punch. These items only require you to use the SKU mix determined in the demand plan to filter down from total demand to the SKU-specific quantity.
3. ***SKU-Specific Adjustables:*** Items that need to be converted from finished products into different units. As such, these are the most complicated to forecast. An example would be Fruit Punch flavor. You will order the flavor in a unit like gallons, kilograms, or pounds. You need to use the BOM to determine how many gallons of flavor are needed to produce the specific quantity of finished goods for that SKU. See the example below and the formulas in the supplemental materials for more details.

Like the supply plan, you will need to complete this monthly, ideally in week 1. You can see that the formulas calculate an ending inventory for the month, which becomes the following month's starting inventory value (i.e. in Jan-26, we finish the month with 33 gallons of Fruit punch flavor, which becomes the beginning value in Feb-26). Before completing the Feb forecast, I recommend checking your inventory system and with the co-packer to confirm how much flavor is actually remaining. Then, adjust your model with the actual number. In this case, we have a theoretical inventory of 33 gallons, but there may only be 30 gallons left (often due to scrap in manufacturing). If your co-packer gives you an updated physical count of 30 gallons, adjust your model to 30 gallons for the forecasting exercise to ensure accurate materials planning. Then, extend your forecast out a month to ensure a rolling 12-month forecast (i.e. during the Feb-26 forecast, I need to add a column for Jan-27 at the end of my model).

Item	*Days per month*	31	28	31	30	31	30
Supply Plan	**Fruit Punch**	**Jan-26**	**Feb-26**	**Mar-26**	**Apr-26**	**May-26**	**Jun-26**
	3. Open PO (Prod Order)	1,200	0	1,000	0	1,300	0
	Grape	**Jan-26**	**Feb-26**	**Mar-26**	**Apr-26**	**May-26**	**Jun-26**
	3. Open PO (Prod Order)	1,000	0	1,000	0	1,200	0
	Pimento Punch	**Jan-26**	**Feb-26**	**Mar-26**	**Apr-26**	**May-26**	**Jun-26**
	3. Open PO (Prod Order)	150	0	220	0	250	0
	Total Cases	**2,350**	**0**	**2,220**	**0**	**2,750**	**0**
MRP	**PKG_16z Bottle**	**Jan-26**	**Feb-26**	**Mar-26**	**Apr-26**	**May-26**	**Jun-26**
Units	1. Inventory	60,000	31,800	71,800	45,160	45,160	72,160
Eaches	2. Production Volume	28,200	0	26,640	0	33,000	0
	3. Open PO	0	40,000	0	0	60,000	0
	4. Ending Inventory	31,800	71,800	45,160	45,160	72,160	72,160
	5. Safety Stock Level	30,000	30,000	30,000	30,000	35,000	35,000
	6. Bottle Coverage	31,800	71,800	45,160	45,160	72,160	72,160
	RM_Fruit Punch Flavor	**Jan-26**	**Feb-26**	**Mar-26**	**Apr-26**	**May-26**	**Jun-26**
Units	1. Inventory	70	33	73	38	38	75
Gallons	2. Production Volume	37	0	35	0	43	0
	3. Open PO	0	40	0	0	80	0
	4. Ending Inventory	33	73	38	38	75	75
	5. Safety Stock Level	40	40	40	40	40	40
	6. Bottle Coverage	12,567	27,805	14,485	14,485	28,461	28,461

One final thought on planning in general. Planning at an early-stage company is really difficult. As noted, you don't have the luxury of leveraging 50 years of data or a sophisticated software tool. You will likely face a point in time when a decision is needed, and you are hesitant to pull the trigger. This makes me recall one of my favorite episodes of *The Sopranos*, where Tony is working with a corrupt councilman on a housing scheme. The councilman is very concerned about how his team is supposed to smuggle copper pipes out of the basement of these lower income homes. Tony taps him on the cheek and says "Councilman: University of Michigan. Harvard Law. Fucking figure it out." That line

31	31	30	31	30	31		
Jul-26	Aug-26	Sep-26	Oct-26	Nov-26	Dec-26	Total Cases	Total Bottles
1,500	0	1,300	0	1,400	0	7,700	92,400
Jul-26	Aug-26	Sep-26	Oct-26	Nov-26	Dec-26	Total Cases	Total Bottles
1,100	0	1,100	0	1,300	0	6,700	80,400
Jul-26	Aug-26	Sep-26	Oct-26	Nov-26	Dec-26	Total Cases	Total Bottles
275	0	300	0	250	0	1,445	17,340
2,875	**0**	**2,700**	**0**	**2,950**	**0**	**15,845**	**190,140**

Jul-26	Aug-26	Sep-26	Oct-26	Nov-26	Dec-26	Total
72,160	37,660	67,660	35,260	35,260	59,860	633,940
34,500	0	32,400	0	35,400	0	190,140
0	30,000	0	0	60,000	0	190,000
37,660	67,660	35,260	35,260	59,860	59,860	52,817
35,000	35,000	35,000	35,000	35,000	35,000	33,333
37,660	67,660	35,260	35,260	59,860	59,860	52,817
Jul-26	Aug-26	Sep-26	Oct-26	Nov-26	Dec-26	Total
75	29	79	37	37	40	625
45	0	43	0	46	0	250
0	50	0	0	50	0	220
29	79	37	37	40	40	50
40	40	40	40	40	40	40
11,211	30,259	14,059	14,059	15,406	15,406	18,888

Abs Min	20,000
Min	30,000
Target	50,000
Max	60,000
Abs Max	75,000

Abs Min	30
Min	40
Target	50
Max	60
Abs Max	70

Figure 7. MRP

perfectly incapsulates many scenarios in a startup company. You can have all the credentials in the world but when it really matters, do you have the skills to make the right decisions and move your company forward? Planning is a great opportunity to demonstrate these skills, but you'll need to adopt the Tony Soprano mentality.

FINANCIAL STATEMENT MODELS

Once all these components are built, your finance team will need to pull them together into a standard, three-statement model (P&L, Balance Sheet, and Cash Flow Forecast). Since you're a Start-Ops leader, there's a good chance you'll be the finance "team" as well in the early stages (along with the supply planner, procurement team, quality department, and manufacturing management)! I did all these jobs in Ritual's first year of operations.

I'm not going to go into an overview of these three financial statements, as you can find a plethora of content online for free (or you can spend six figures to learn it in B-school like me; maybe start with the online videos)! I will show you how to use your demand plan, supply plan, and MRP to forecast projected cash flows. This is probably the most crucial financial activity of an early-stage startup and the most important model for your investors.

The Cash Flow Forecast

It follows a logical process:

1. Use the demand plan x average revenue per unit or case to calculate revenue.
2. Use the supply plan and the MRP to calculate cash needs to build inventory.
3. Use your budget for A&P (advertising and promotion), which will capture sales and marketing costs.
4. Layer in some G&A projections (general and administrative).

One nuance involves using cash accounting vs accrual accounting. In cash accounting, you account for costs when they are incurred; in accrual accounting, you account for the costs when the product is sold. For example, if you place a PO for glass bottles to be delivered in March, cash accounting models that cost hitting the P&L in March. Accrual accounting has the cash outflow hit the P&L via COGS at the time when the product is sold (so a rolling period until all those bottles are sold). See below for a practical example of this process. As mentioned in the intro, this type of exercise is challenging to describe in words. See the ***Cash Flow Forecast*** in the supplemental spreadsheets, Figure 8 below, and look for demos on ***The Start-Ops Playbook*** YouTube channel.

CASH IN	1/4	1/11	1/18	1/25	2/1
Current Cash	$2,000,000.00	$1,804,700.00	$1,609,400.00	$1,414,100.00	$1,218,800.00
AR Collect	$200,000.00	$0.00	$0.00	$200,000.00	$0.00
Projected remaining net sales	$30,000.00	$30,000.00	$30,000.00	$30,000.00	$30,000.00
INVESTMENT	$0.00	$0.00	$0.00	$0.00	$0.00
TOTAL CASH IN	**$2,230,000.00**	**$1,834,700.00**	**$1,639,400.00**	**$1,644,100.00**	**$1,248,800.00**
Budget Expenses					
Production					
Material	$70,000.00	$70,000.00	$70,000.00	$70,000.00	$70,000.00
Labor	$45,000.00	$45,000.00	$45,000.00	$45,000.00	$45,000.00
A&P					
Marketing					
Agency Fees	$6,250.00	$6,250.00	$6,250.00	$6,250.00	$6,250.00
Asset Creation	$4,875.00	$4,875.00	$4,875.00	$4,875.00	$4,875.00
Digital Media	$25,000.00	$25,000.00	$25,000.00	$25,000.00	$25,000.00
Paid Search	$20,000.00	$20,000.00	$20,000.00	$20,000.00	$20,000.00
Tactical / Opportunity	$6,625.00	$6,625.00	$6,625.00	$6,625.00	$6,625.00
Sales					
Off-Premise Support	$6,500.00	$6,500.00	$6,500.00	$6,500.00	$6,500.00
On-Premise Support	$2,750.00	$2,750.00	$2,750.00	$2,750.00	$2,750.00
Ecomm Support Agency	$0.00	$0.00	$0.00	$0.00	$0.00
Trade Shows / Events	$500.00	$500.00	$500.00	$500.00	$500.00
Tactical / Opportunity	$2,500.00	$2,500.00	$2,500.00	$2,500.00	$2,500.00
G&A					
Payroll					
Salary	$20,000.00	$20,000.00	$20,000.00	$20,000.00	$20,000.00
Taxes & Fees	$5,800.00	$5,800.00	$5,800.00	$5,800.00	$5,800.00
Health Insurance	$6,500.00	$6,500.00	$6,500.00	$6,500.00	$6,500.00
Contractors	$0.00	$0.00	$0.00	$0.00	$0.00
Operations					
Accounting & Inventory Mgmt	$2,000.00	$2,000.00	$2,000.00	$2,000.00	$2,000.00
IT & Software	$5,000.00	$5,000.00	$5,000.00	$5,000.00	$5,000.00
Legal & Compliance	$2,000.00	$2,000.00	$2,000.00	$2,000.00	$2,000.00
Office Supplies & Expenses	$500.00	$500.00	$500.00	$500.00	$500.00
Outsourced Merch Support	$0.00	$0.00	$0.00	$0.00	$0.00
Outsourced Sales Team	$0.00	$0.00	$0.00	$0.00	$0.00
Recruiting Costs	$0.00	$0.00	$0.00	$0.00	$0.00
Rent	$3,000.00	$3,000.00	$3,000.00	$3,000.00	$3,000.00
Research & Development	$5,000.00	$5,000.00	$5,000.00	$5,000.00	$5,000.00
Shipping / Sampling	$2,000.00	$2,000.00	$2,000.00	$2,000.00	$2,000.00
Travel & Entertainment	$3,000.00	$3,000.00	$3,000.00	$3,000.00	$3,000.00
Utilities/Insurance	$500.00	$500.00	$500.00	$500.00	$500.00
Discretionary	$0.00	$0.00	$0.00	$0.00	$0.00
TOTAL BUDGET EXPENSES	**$245,300.00**	**$245,300.00**	**$245,300.00**	**$245,300.00**	**$245,300.00**
OTHER PAYABLES					
AP Out	$200,000.00	$0.00	$0.00	$200,000.00	$0.00
N/A	$0.00	$0.00	$0.00	$0.00	$0.00
N/A	$0.00	$0.00	$0.00	$0.00	$0.00
N/A	$0.00	$0.00	$0.00	$0.00	$0.00
TOTAL OTHER COSTS	**$200,000.00**	**$0.00**	**$0.00**	**$200,000.00**	**$0.00**
TOTAL CASH OUT	**$445,300.00**	**$245,300.00**	**$245,300.00**	**$445,300.00**	**$245,300.00**
ENDING CASH	**$1,784,700.00**	**$1,569,400.00**	**$1,354,100.00**	**$1,138,800.00**	**$923,500.00**

2/8	2/15	2/22	3/1	3/8	3/15	3/22
$1,023,500.00	**$828,200.00**	**$632,900.00**	**$437,600.00**	**$242,300.00**	**$1,547,000.00**	**$1,551,700.00**
$0.00	$200,000.00	$0.00	$0.00	$200,000.00	$200,000.00	$200,000.00
$30,000.00	$30,000.00	$30,000.00	$30,000.00	$30,000.00	$30,000.00	$30,000.00
$0.00	$0.00	$0.00	$0.00	**$1,500,000.00**	$0.00	$0.00
$1,053,500.00	**$1,058,200.00**	**$662,900.00**	**$467,600.00**	**$1,972,300.00**	**$1,777,000.00**	**$1,781,700.00**
$70,000.00	$70,000.00	$70,000.00	$70,000.00	$70,000.00	$70,000.00	$70,000.00
$45,000.00	$45,000.00	$45,000.00	$45,000.00	$45,000.00	$45,000.00	$45,000.00
$6,250.00	$6,250.00	$6,250.00	$6,250.00	$6,250.00	$6,250.00	$6,250.00
$4,875.00	$4,875.00	$4,875.00	$4,875.00	$4,875.00	$4,875.00	$4,875.00
$25,000.00	$25,000.00	$25,000.00	$25,000.00	$25,000.00	$25,000.00	$25,000.00
$20,000.00	$20,000.00	$20,000.00	$20,000.00	$20,000.00	$20,000.00	$20,000.00
$6,625.00	$6,625.00	$6,625.00	$6,625.00	$6,625.00	$6,625.00	$6,625.00
$6,500.00	$6,500.00	$6,500.00	$6,500.00	$6,500.00	$6,500.00	$6,500.00
$2,750.00	$2,750.00	$2,750.00	$2,750.00	$2,750.00	$2,750.00	$2,750.00
$0.00	$0.00	$0.00	$0.00	$0.00	$0.00	$0.00
$500.00	$500.00	$500.00	$500.00	$500.00	$500.00	$500.00
$2,500.00	$2,500.00	$2,500.00	$2,500.00	$2,500.00	$2,500.00	$2,500.00
$20,000.00	$20,000.00	$20,000.00	$20,000.00	$20,000.00	$20,000.00	$20,000.00
$5,800.00	$5,800.00	$5,800.00	$5,800.00	$5,800.00	$5,800.00	$5,800.00
$6,500.00	$6,500.00	$6,500.00	$6,500.00	$6,500.00	$6,500.00	$6,500.00
$0.00	$0.00	$0.00	$0.00	$0.00	$0.00	$0.00
$2,000.00	$2,000.00	$2,000.00	$2,000.00	$2,000.00	$2,000.00	$2,000.00
$5,000.00	$5,000.00	$5,000.00	$5,000.00	$5,000.00	$5,000.00	$5,000.00
$2,000.00	$2,000.00	$2,000.00	$2,000.00	$2,000.00	$2,000.00	$2,000.00
$500.00	$500.00	$500.00	$500.00	$500.00	$500.00	$500.00
$0.00	$0.00	$0.00	$0.00	$0.00	$0.00	$0.00
$0.00	$0.00	$0.00	$0.00	$0.00	$0.00	$0.00
$0.00	$0.00	$0.00	$0.00	$0.00	$0.00	$0.00
$3,000.00	$3,000.00	$3,000.00	$3,000.00	$3,000.00	$3,000.00	$3,000.00
$5,000.00	$5,000.00	$5,000.00	$5,000.00	$5,000.00	$5,000.00	$5,000.00
$2,000.00	$2,000.00	$2,000.00	$2,000.00	$2,000.00	$2,000.00	$2,000.00
$3,000.00	$3,000.00	$3,000.00	$3,000.00	$3,000.00	$3,000.00	$3,000.00
$500.00	$500.00	$500.00	$500.00	$500.00	$500.00	$500.00
$0.00	$0.00	$0.00	$0.00	$0.00	$0.00	$0.00
$245,300.00	**$245,300.00**	**$245,300.00**	**$245,300.00**	**$245,300.00**	**$245,300.00**	**$245,300.00**
$0.00	$200,000.00	$0.00	$0.00	$200,000.00	$0.00	$0.00
$0.00	$0.00	$0.00	$0.00	$0.00	$0.00	$0.00
$0.00	$0.00	$0.00	$0.00	$0.00	$0.00	$0.00
$0.00	$0.00	$0.00	$0.00	$0.00	$0.00	$0.00
$0.00	**$200,000.00**	**$0.00**	**$0.00**	**$200,000.00**	**$0.00**	**$0.00**
$245,300.00	**$445,300.00**	**$245,300.00**	**$245,300.00**	**$445,300.00**	**$245,300.00**	**$245,300.00**
$708,200.00	**$492,900.00**	**$277,600.00**	**$62,300.00**	**$1,347,000.00**	**$1,331,700.00**	**$1,316,400.00**

Figure 8. Cash Flow Forecast

That's a wrap for pillar 1. Hopefully we learned, laughed, and maybe pissed and moaned a bit about the MRP. I'm structuring this as a practical guide you can refer back to on the job. One of my heroes, economist and philosopher Murray Rothbard, used to say: "Theory needs to work in Practice. Anyone who ever said 'it works on paper but fails in practice,' actually just screwed up on the paper". Here are a few quick facts to give you some benchmarks.

1-C. The Wrap: Quick Facts for Benchmarks

Factor	Benchmark
Formulation	Typically structured in 1,000 Gal for liquids.
BOM creation	Adjust batch volumes down to qty of each ingredient to produce a single unit.
Planning schedule and Tools	Create 3–5 year demand plan, complete with P&L, Balance Sheet, and Cash Flow forecast.
Cash raises	Use your demand plan, P&L, and cash flow projections to forecast annual cash needs, which will likely culminate in an annual investor review to raise more cash.
Low-cost ERP options	Cin7 Core, Acumatica, Workday, Epicor
ERP cost	$2-5K per year
Accounting resources	Find an external accounting service like Belay (formerly Accountfully) to manage your internal accounting. https://www.accountfully.com/
Monthly Accounting spend	Depending on the services, this could be $2-8K per month.
Demand plan accuracy	Your forecast should be within +/- 20% of actuals or you need to adjust your approach.
Inventory DOH target (days on hand)	3-4 months of inventory for longer shelf-life items (>1 year). 2 months is ideal if you have a flexible contract manufacturer.
MRP excess	Add 20% safety factor to your material planning.

PILLAR 2

PROCUREMENT

2-A. The Situation: Setting the Scene

Picture the stereotypical Ops resource. What are you seeing? Is it a nerdy guy with thick glasses, thinning hair, and an affinity for reading dense non-fiction about the failures of government? Well, some stereotypes exist for a reason. There's nothing particularly glamorous about engineers who work in manufacturing plants or designers who work in a lab.

Fresh out of college, I remember living in Hoboken with my finance-bro friends who worked in the city. They would throw on their suits and attend events called "galas" (still not sure what these are), while I hauled it forty-five minutes down the NJ turnpike to a dirty plant in dreary south Jersey. While most of the typical operations roles are conducted in plants, warehouses, and labs, there is one exception, where we finally get to step into the boardroom: enter procurement.

Procurement involves the purchase of raw and packaging materials needed to produce your product. If you have a beverage company, you will need to buy cans, bottles, caps, corks, labels, and boxes. If it's food, you will need cartons, containers, tubes, sleeves, etc. You'll also need to purchase all the raw materials associated with your formulation, which can be challenging and costly.

One of my favorite aspects of being a startup operator has always been working with suppliers to build relationships and negotiate contracts. At Ritual, I became so passionate about reducing our material costs, I coined the acronym "ABQ" (always be quoting) and challenged our team to adopt this mentality. However, procurement is not all sunshine and butterflies. Let's review the keys to building a durable, sustainable, and cost-effective material network.

2-B. The Core: Section Contents

- Objective: How to create a database of reliable suppliers and negotiate the lowest material cost
- Key Components:
  - Catalog of Suppliers
  - Negotiation Strategy
  - RFP
  - Contracts

CATALOG OF SUPPLIERS

Before you can start buying anything, you'll need a robust list of suppliers. Think of this exercise as building a catalog, with as many appropriate suppliers as you can find. In addition to simple online searches, leverage contacts in the industry. Identify your friends who work in CPG and ask them who their supplier is for various types of packaging. Find out any other companies they've worked with in the past. Start constructing a list that looks like Figure 9 below:

Type	Item	Supplier	Lead Time	Origin	Alternate Supplier	Origin
Pkg	Bottles	Supplier A1	120+ days	China	Supplier A2	Eastern EU
Pkg	Caps	Supplier B1	120+ days	Mexico	Supplier B2	Italy
Pkg	Labels	Supplier C1	30-60 days	USA	Supplier C2	USA
Pkg	Corrugate	Supplier D1	30-60 days	USA	Supplier D2	USA
Pkg	Tamper Evident Seal	Supplier E1	120+ days	USA	N/A	N/A
Raw	Flavor Concentrate	Supplier F1	30 days	USA	N/A	N/A
Raw	Sugar, Salt, other raws	Supplier G1	15-30 days	USA	Supplier G2	USA

Figure 9. Supplier Catalog

Note that not all vendors, including the most reputable names in the industry, may be appropriate for supplying a startup company. Some key factors when selecting an appropriate vendor are detailed below.

The Supplier Catalog

Key factors:

1. ***MOQ (minimum order quantities)***: You'll want to understand what the supplier's minimum order quantity is to fulfill an order. The bigger the company, the bigger the MOQ. I had a tamper evident capsule supplier who refused to supply us with anything less than 500,000 capsules per run.
2. ***Lead Times***: Get a firm commitment on how quickly these items can be delivered. Your production run schedule, detailed in the prior section, will need to factor in the longest lead-time items, which can run up to 6 months (i.e. glass bottles usually originate in SE Asia or Eastern Europe and need to be ordered 6 months in advance of delivery).
3. ***Material Origin***: What is the country of origin for your supplier's materials? Do the economically illiterate bozos in D.C. consider this country a "threat" to America, by providing us lower cost material, which translates to lower

cost goods, which translates to more disposable income for the lowest income Americans? (Spoiler alert: I prefer free trade to destructive tariffs.) Also, what is the level of geo-political stability in this country? We can all appreciate a good revolution to overhaul a totalitarian government, but let's make sure it doesn't screw up my production run.

4. ***Price:*** Obvious, but we'll dive into a lot more detail on how to negotiate the lowest price from a position of minimal power.

NEGOTIATION STRATEGY

Now that you're armed with a robust list of suppliers, it's time to prepare for a negotiation. Negotiations are a bit of an art-science combination, so you'll need to develop your own approach. Here are a few thoughts on how I developed my strategy. The bulk of it is derived from Victoria Medvec's stellar book ***Negotiate Without Fear***. You're knee deep in a technical operations manual, and I'm giving you another non-fiction guide to read immediately afterward? Yes, that sucks. Having said that, buy, read, and absorb her book. Another key point is on the modern mentality of negotiations. People think of great negotiators as these assholes like ***Wall Street's*** Gordon Gekko in $10,000 suits, threatening someone's family if they don't make the deal. In reality, the best negotiators are typically the most creative people in the room. They are the deeply prepared leaders who spend countless hours researching the counterparty to understand their desires, capabilities, strengths, and weaknesses. They are also the people with the courage to take a shot at an unconventional arrangement, or ask for just a little bit more, without worrying about offending someone.

The Negotiation Strategy

We'll start with a framework and expand on the winning techniques:

1. *Research and Objectives*: Build background knowledge of the counter-party's goals and capabilities.
2. *Negotiable Points:* Develop a multi-faceted list of negotiable points for the meeting.
3. *The Terms:* Settle on a BATNA and reservation point.
4. *RFP:* Submit a request for proposal (detailed below).
5. *The Offer:* Create an ambitious offer.
6. *Sealing the Deal:* Concessions and contracts (also detailed more below).

You can find ample materials to expand on these steps, notably *Negotiate Without Fear,* as mentioned above. I will add a bit of personal depth on creating a list of negotiable points, conducting the RFP, and crafting a robust contract.

NEGOTIABLE POINTS

One of the key takeaways from *Negotiate Without Fear* is the need to develop a robust list of negotiable points prior to entering the negotiation. The common mistake is to arrive at a negotiation ready to barter over price. Dr. Medvec refers to price as a ***contentious issue*** (i.e. issues in which you want the opposite of your counterparty; I want a low price, they want a high price). Her recommendation is to build a suite of negotiable issues to include as part of a comprehensive discussion; price becomes part of the discussion but is embedded in a much more holistic relationship. This was one of the most effective strategies I deployed in the early days of Ritual. See Figure 10 for examples of items I would mix and match in my negotiations.

Beyond ***contentious issues***, also prepare ***storyboard*** and ***tradeoff issues***. Map your needs/desires vs the counterparties on a grid of issues important to you and important to them. A ***trade-off issue*** is something important to them, but fairly inconsequential to you. For me, delivery date was an item I was able to flex on. Most brands want to receive goods just-in-time (JIT). This was less of an issue for us because of our financing plan (we had a reliable, annual cycle of cash infusion). As a result, there were times when I would receive packaging materials one to two months before I needed them. The supplier likes this because it provides them with a more predictable schedule of cash-flows. In return, they provided a lower piece price. A ***storyboard issue*** is a win-win. These are very powerful in negotiations. I would arrive with customer referrals, future projects, and a detailed volume-tier price plan. They love to see you are thinking about dramatically increasing your volume, so the suppliers tend to be much more willing to talk price breaks when you show them growth curve.

The key to mapping these issues is a detailed research phase. Hit the company's website, read about their strategy, and shape your points accordingly. In one example, I led the negotiation by pointing out a new service line from my supplier that I was interested in purchasing; the service was so new, my rep wasn't even aware his company had this offering! This dramatically increases your credibility in a negotiation by showing you are prepared, know the alternate offerings, and are willing to build a comprehensive partnership. Pick one of your suppliers, do a little research, and try to map the Figure 10 grid for your materials.

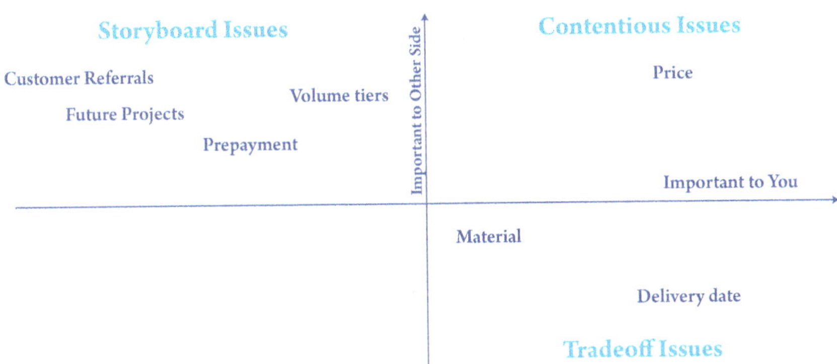

Figure 10. Negotiable Point Framework from "Negotiate Without Fear"

RFP (REQUEST FOR PROPOSAL)

Once you are further along in your company's history (think year two or three), you can start to build out a list of demands and submit an RFP. That's right: even a startup company with limited revenue can afford to be picky. After all, in this case, you're the customer, and the customer is always right (even though most of the time, the customer is an asshole or a moron—see Larry David's rant from an ice cream shop altercation in ***Curb***). RFP stands for request for proposal, which is essentially a packet of materials sent in bulk to a large database of suppliers. It enables you to rapidly assemble a portfolio of bids from alternate suppliers. Think of it like Lebron on a free agent tour. Do you want to be in South Beach, SoCal, or the majestic streets of NE Ohio (my hometown)?

The RFP

A quality RFP consists of 11 sections (it's a lot, but once you build it, your part is done):

1. ***Background:*** Details on your company history, the project objectives, scope, and timing.
2. ***Scope***: Detailed version of what the supplier will supply. This includes specifications on your materials, delivery locations, and lead time targets.
3. ***Company Information:*** The supplier will enter details on their company history, revenue, employees, supply chain, and customer references.
4. ***Capabilities & Expertise:*** Description of what the supplier can offer, different types of materials available, specifications and limitations of their materials, sizes of containers, certifications, and regulatory compliance.
5. ***Service:*** Lead times, quality metrics, customer service details, and value-added services.
6. ***IT Systems & Tech:*** Systems used for managing orders, receiving purchase orders, and sending invoices.
7. ***Business Continuity Plan:*** Plans if a natural disaster hits the production facility and methods to ensure data security.
8. ***Pricing:*** Section where price bids are submitted.
9. ***Additional Discounts:*** Rebate offers, discounts for achieving various volume tiers, signing bonuses, and payment terms.
10. ***Terms & Conditions:*** Basic contract parameters (detailed more below).
11. ***Questions & Comments:*** Leave a blank section so the supplier can add any questions for you.

This does require a lot of back and forth with the vendors, so you may want to outsource the RFP management. It is a small investment that comes with almost immediate ROI. I worked with some folks in Indonesia who did a terrific job for us. Their website is listed here: (https://dpoandco.com/bpo). Once the RFP is complete, revert to the previous section and apply all the same negotiation framework as you work to seal the deal. Rank order the proposals, incorporating qualitative factors, like whether you enjoy working with this supplier or if the account rep is an asshole. Don't discount the importance of avoiding doing business with pricks to save a couple pennies. I can guarantee that problems will arise with virtually every material you buy at some point in the company's lifecycle. When this inevitably happens, it's crucial that you have a partner you can trust to actively work towards a solution. The two cents you saved after the RFP disappear rapidly when you receive one bad batch of materials, and the supplier refuses to take responsibility for the defective product.

The RFP is the single most effective strategy I found at Ritual for reducing our costs. Not only do you gain leverage with a supplier by referencing another supplier offering a better price, but it's also an educational experience for you as a leader. You get a great sense of what other suppliers are offering, which ones are at the cutting edge of the industry, and which ones are struggling to survive. Education is the currency we trade in with Operations. One of my favorite quotes is from Mark Twain: "Don't you kids let ***School*** get in the way of your ***Education.***" That's damn right. Adopt a mentality of continuous learning or fall behind the competition.

One item to note: an RFP is not for everyone. You need to have large enough volumes to justify the supplier's time filling out this detailed packet. You should get a sense of that from the conversations you've had with various suppliers. If you're not sure whether an RFP is appropriate, just remember, there are no negative points in RFPs. If your current supplier is offended that you want to bid out the business, that supplier clearly doesn't understand market economics. They are like Dennis Reynolds in ***It's Always Sunny in Philadelphia***: "I don't understand how the U.S economy works; frankly, I don't understand how finance works." Competition is part of the game and anyone who doesn't want to compete is not someone I want in my foxhole.

Review the RFP template and think about what additions you should include to customize it for your business.

CONTRACTS

We're in the home stretch. You've built a database of suppliers. You put out an RFP and negotiated a great deal to ensure durable supply for years to come. Now, it's time to paper the agreement. I highly recommend working with a business attorney and papering agreements with all your suppliers.

In my first few years, I had several handshake agreements. Back to the intro—recall that Ritual's first year in operations was 2020. The global economy was shuttered in an unprecedented and unsustainable manner. The expectation was we could print up a bunch of money and hand it out to all the people not producing for an indefinite period of time. This is obviously economic nonsense: when you send out checks—in many cases 2-3x larger than these people were making in their regular jobs—it increases demand. Do this while simultaneously stifling supply, and you have an inflation timebomb on your hands.

By June 2020, I had a solid grasp of what was going to happen to prices in 2021 and made an aggressive decision to issue purchase orders for the next 14-18 months. One supplier was happy to accept these POs, which is a formal agreement to supply the material at the agreed upon volumes, timeframe, and price.

Our arrangement was proceeding according to plan, with the price lock guarantee and bottles arriving on time. However, when the inevitable inflation started to hit the market in the form of >10% PPI and ~8% CPI (according to the Fed, which drastically underestimates inflation), the supplier started to balk. They started sending me price increase letters from their manufacturer (i.e. my supplier was a distributor of this material for an original manufacturer). I read the price increase letters and thought "well, it sucks to be you!" But eventually the supplier refused to honor my pricing. Even though I had accurately forecasted the inflation and taken appropriate precautions, I didn't have a robust contract guaranteeing the price lock for a set duration. Several months later, we had a quality issue with the material and the already tenuous relationship with this supplier completely dissolved. I learned a valuable lesson in this exchange: no matter how solid your relationship with a supplier seems, always document the agreed-upon terms.

A lot of people think of contracts like signing the terms and conditions when you get a new phone: scroll to the bottom and tell me where to sign. Leave it to the lawyers and, dare I say, ***trust the experts***. This mentality shows a fundamental misunderstanding of what a good contract ought to be. Yes, I do recommend the support of lawyers to draft up the core of a contract. But it is your responsibility to ensure the primary factors in the relationship are captured in that contract. If you haven't sat with the lawyer to review a list of critical items you discussed with the supplier, then you probably haven't done your part in ensuring a quality contract is developed. Your contract will need to be referenced frequently over time, so it's crucial to invest the time upfront and align on something practical, measurable, and achievable.

One other key point is the concept of ***mutualism***. I interviewed with the Mars company during business school, and while I decided to move into consulting, I was very impressed with the Mars principles. The most impactful item on the list is that of ***mutualism***, which means Mars is committed to ensuring mutually beneficial relationships with its suppliers and customers. While the free market naturally encourages mutualistic relationships, it was refreshing to see the commitment Mars had to instill this principle into daily operations. Conventional wisdom on negotiations says you win when your supplier loses. The great Thomas Sowell points out in his masterpiece ***Basic Economics*** that most economic fallacies are grounded in viewing the world as a zero-sum game. "Tricking" a supplier into signing a malicious contract doesn't do anyone any good in the long run. Again, you might save a few pennies on one shipment, but good luck getting your caps last second the first time you make a forecasting error (yes, even with section one of this playbook, forecasting is really hard). Work with your supplier to develop a mutually beneficial and incredibly explicit contract detailing the core components of your relationship. You wouldn't sign a marriage license without asking your soon-to-be spouse if they want kids (or at least you shouldn't). Don't execute a contract with inequity and impracticality built in by design.

The Contract

The key components of a contract are as follows:

1. *Terms:* How long are we agreeing to keep this contract in place? When can we void it? What is required to be purchased? How will the supplier be paid?

2. ***Scenarios:*** What could go wrong and how are we going to manage the financial, legal, and administrative responsibilities when something goes wrong?
3. ***Pricing and Discounts***: What is the pricing structure for POs (purchase orders)? When can we earn discounts and how will they be applied?
4. ***Exclusivity***: Can we work with competitors or is this an exclusive relationship?
5. ***Insurance and Ownership***: Who will cover what and at what point in our relationship? When does ownership of material transfer?
6. ***And a Bunch of Legal Mumbo-Jumbo***: Indemnification, force majeure, severability, and several other 'ilities. Turn this over to the lawyers.

2-C. The Wrap: Quick Facts for Benchmarks

That's a wrap for pillar two. If you remember just one thing from this chapter, it's the importance of striking a balance between the ABQ mentality and building a relationship of mutualism. ABQ is about external curiosity. Markets move quickly, so you should be constantly gauging fluctuations in commodity prices, labor rates, insurance costs, interest rates, and even international trade laws. Each of these items will impact your supply reliability and cost. As my dad always said, "you need to have two bites of the apple." In procurement, I don't think that goes far enough. You need an apple, an orange, and maybe even a kiwi.

You need to understand that supplier relationships are paramount to your brand's success. It's amazing how far the fundamentals can extend. Several very simple, zero-cost activities can go a long way to cementing mutually beneficial, long-term relationships. Providing your supplier with a reliable forecast is step one. Remember, your supplier is running a business too, usually with much lower margins. Inventory management and cash flow are some of their most important KPIs, so an accurate forecast with sufficient runway for purchase and delivery will make your supplier love working with you. Also, respond to their quotes. If they didn't win the bid, explain why and be truthful. "Your prices exceeded our budget" or "the minimum quantities were too high" are perfectly acceptable answers. "It's not you, it's me…wait a minute, no, it is you".

Lastly, take a word of wisdom from Big Worm in the movie ***Friday***: "Playing with my money is like playing with my emotions!" This means **pay your suppliers on time**. The U.S. Government has a mantra: "We always pay our bills." Peter Schiff, my favorite modern economist, points out the irony, considering our $38T in debt has accumulated precisely because we never pay our bills! Don't be the U.S. Government. Ensure timely payments with your suppliers. Work closely with your accounting team to build a reliable process, including avenues for exception payments (i.e. same day wires) in special cases. A supplier who can trust in on-time payment will bend over backwards to support you in a crunch.

Now, let's review a few benchmarks:

Factor	Benchmark
# of suppliers in an RFP	At least 3, 10-15 is an ideal number. Enough to establish a reliable range, but not too many to dig deep into the capabilities.
Minimum volume for RFP	For packaging items around 500K is probably the minimum to attract bids. 1M per year with steady growth is an ideal #.
Length of contracts	I like 2-year contracts with annual price reviews. I also insert "not to exceed" price raises of ~5% in the next year price review.
% split between suppliers	I recommend a dual source model on critical, long-lead items. You should source ~90% with your primary supplier and ~10% with the secondary supplier. For example, if you get 6 deliveries per year, have 5 of them with your primary supplier and 1 with your backup.
Negotiation levers	Key levers to use in negotiations: • Reference RFP data • Use payment terms for discounts • Price tiers at various volume thresholds • Rebates at annual volume targets

PILLAR 3

QUALITY

3-A. The Situation: Setting the Scene

Let's take another trip back to spring 2020. Ritual was just getting off the ground and I had established a few basic operating standards (mostly the first two pillars). It was clearly time to start expanding our operational program. We had limited resources, limited budget, and little room for error. In my infinite wisdom, I selected the obvious, critical area of focus: Power BI dashboarding! I had seen some very cool, flashy reporting in my last gig and was sure we needed to get something like that in place. Unfortunately, I didn't know how to build these models—but how hard could it be? After all, our investor is going to be blown away with these pretty charts. I went down a rabbit hole of YouTube videos, learned enough to be adequate, and built some pretty decent reports. Our investor was pleased with the tool, but it did very little to drive day-to-day business decisions. Meanwhile, a glaring gap that could threaten the very existence of any business was sitting in the closet, getting as much attention as a 15-year old putter. What we really needed was a Commercial Quality System (CQS).

It should go without saying that product quality is paramount—the most important component of an operational leader's agenda in consumer products (I find it slightly ironic that the phrase "it goes without saying" always seems to precede the most important things anyone can say). First, consumer safety is on the line and in your hands. That's right: if someone gets hurt by one of your products, it's on you, the Ops leader. This is a responsibility you need to take very seriously from day one. While this might sound a little daunting, we're going to walk through the core components and establish all the baseline needs. You'll need to get a support network in place so as not to shoulder the burden alone. This is another time to lean on industry experts, and I'll guide you on how to identify the people who know what the hell they're talking about.

3-B. The Core: Section Contents

- Objective: How to build a Commercial Quality System (CQS)
- Key Components:
  - Operating Procedures and Testing
  - Compliance Documentation
  - Manufacturing Standards

OPERATING PROCEDURES AND TESTING

I'm the type of leader who puts a lot of stock into words and actions; I don't like to waste time with red tape and fluff. A key reason I left the consulting world was I got tired of building useless PowerPoint decks full of recommendations that I wasn't personally responsible for implementing. Quick sidebar about consulting that I think is important when thinking about entrepreneurship: here's a great clip of Steve Jobs explaining why consulting sucks (see QR code below). When you watch this clip, why is it so funny? It's the core of most great stand-up comedy routines. What he's saying is so unequivocally true, but we're supposed to pretend like you can't say it out loud. Even the consultants in the room are laughing, as if Jobs is providing some good-natured ribbing. Hey folks: he's serious! He doesn't respect your career choice.

As I previously mentioned, I hate binary thinking and believe it's at the root of so many of the fallacies in our society. However, there is such a distinct difference in the ownership component of business strategy that I think you are either a consultant or an entrepreneur. You really need to pick one and I'm thrilled with the choice I made. I expect many of the readers are in business school or early in their careers. Many of you are probably considering both fields (as I was in B-school). Make sure you take enough time to understand the differences between these two diametrically opposed career paths. Back to the task at hand. I bring this up because, while I don't typically put a ton of merit into pure documentation and credentials, quality is one very clear exception. Your quality system is only as valid as what you can prove was completed, and the foundation of your CQS is a detailed operating manual.

The Operating Manual

The operating manual should detail how to make your product and the acceptable release limits:

1. ***Processing Specifications and Procedures:*** Details how to batch, blend, treat, and fill the product.
2. ***Packaging Specifications:*** Specifies limitations on aesthetics and functionality of each packaging component.

3. *Sampling*: Outlines test quantities and procedures.
4. *Analytical Testing*: Provides thresholds for product release on lab test parameters.
5. *Sensory Testing:* Establishes protocols and criteria for product release on subjective parameters, including taste, texture, visual, aroma, mouth feel, etc.

The components to the operating manual are not very intuitive so let's zoom into each one in more detail. I also included the ***Operating Manual*** in the supplemental materials for review:

1. *Processing Specs and Procedures*: Referring back to the bill of materials section, you'll recall the discussion on collaborating with your formula designer. As part of their package of deliverables, they should provide a detailed manual for producing at scale. This manual should include each of the following subcomponents:
   i. *Production Formula*: A list of the items to produce the formula at scale (shown back in Figure 1).
   ii. *Blending Instructions*: How much of each ingredient to add, the sequence of additions, length of mixing time, temperatures, etc.
   iii. *Product Specifications*: Parameters including brix, specific gravity, density, fill level, etc. and the allowable range.
   iv. *Other Processing Instructions*: Treatment procedures like tunnel pasteurization should be specified by the time, temperature, and pasteurization unit requirements.

2. ***Packaging Specs:*** Packaging specs should provide requirements on the position and fit of your packaging items:
    i. ***Material Presence:*** List out all the items included in your BOM, which need to be verified in manufacturing.
    ii. ***Closures/Lids:*** Identify how the lid, cap, etc. need to sit when properly applied
    iii. ***Lot code format:*** Identify the date, shift, facility and batch number for when and where the product was produced. This is used for traceability and will become critical if quality defects are found in the field or during a site audit/certification. For example, if it was produced in the Mansfield plant, line 2, February 15th, 2025, the lot code might read: MAN25042LN2 001 (Manfield plant, year YY, Julian date [42 day of the year], Line 2, batch #1). You will need to specify in the operating manual all the places where the Lot code must appear, size, color, etc.
    iv. ***Label Placement:*** Identify where a properly placed label must sit on your container.
    v. ***Best By Date/Expiration:*** Near the lot code, you may need to add a "Best By" date. This should be determined in tandem with your formula developer using shelf-life testing. The product is inserted into a hot box, which accelerates the aging process and provides a projected shelf-life (i.e. if you need 12 months of shelf life, this can be determined after ~3 months in a hot box). If you learn your product has a 12-month shelf-life, code your product as "Best By" one year from the date of production.
3. ***Sampling***: Highlight the number of samples needed per batch for analytical testing. A typical process might be one sample

every x hours (i.e. you might pull one sample every two hours, run for 10 hours, and collect five samples per batch).

4. *Analytical Testing*: Specify each analytical test to be conducted and the allowable range for compliant product. Common tests include:
   i. APC (Aerobic Plate Count) — Measures total bacterial activity
   ii. Yeast
   iii. Mold
   iv. Lactic Acid Bacteria
   v. Acetic Acid Bacteria
   vi. pH (how acidic or alkaline the material is, ranging from 0-14)
5. *Sensory Testing:* You will need to specify how the product needs to taste, look, smell, and the overall product experience. This is typically done by building a gold-standard reference sample. Then, develop tasting protocols and train the appropriate staff members to conduct the sensory.

And that is your operating manual. This document is particularly crucial when you are working with contract manufacturers. Remember, no one is going to care as much about your product as you, so it is imperative that you specify acceptable vs. unacceptable in painstaking detail.

COMPLIANCE DOCUMENTATION

Admit it: you've been waiting for this section like you've been waiting for another season of *The Sopranos*. As lame and bureaucratic as this may sound on the surface, compliance documentation in CPG actually does serve a purpose! These documents need to be customized to the business, the product, and the production facility. As a result, when building these documents, you will be rubbing elbows with industry experts who will teach you a tremendous amount about improving quality. They will also help to train and improve your existing production facilities (again, this is especially true in contract manufacturing). Here are the documents needed as table stakes for the CQS:

1. ***GFSI Certification:*** This stands for the Good Food Safety Initiative. It is a type of third-party certification on your manufacturing site's standards.
2. ***Process Authority Letter:*** Letter from a third-party process expert validating he/she has reviewed the process and authorizes the production as specified in the operating manual.
3. ***Food Safety and Food Defense Plans:*** Specification of hazards, critical control points, and risk mitigation strategies. Food safety refers to product related issues (i.e. pathogen contamination), while food defense refers to defending your product from tampering (i.e. how you will control the people with access to your product).
4. ***Challenge Study:*** These are lab tests to determine how resistant your product is against pathogens and spoilage.
5. ***Commercial Quality Audits:*** Third-party led audits for verification of quality standards.
6. ***Certificate of Analysis (CoA):*** Accompanying documentation for receiving materials to validate required tests were completed prior to arrival.

Again, let's take a closer look at the underlying documents:

1. ***GFSI Certification:*** We have an entire section in our future on contract manufacturing, so this can serve as a preview. One piece of documentation needed from a co-packer is the GFSI certification. This is effectively a market-driven, third-party validation, confirming the production site meets industry standards. It is a retailer driven initiative, required by all the major retailers, including Walmart, Target, and Costco. There are several different acceptable third-party certifiers, including BRC, SQF, and FSSC. The co-packer should provide this certification during the scoping phase (covered in pillar four).
2. ***Process Authority Letter (PAL):*** If you've ever heard anyone ask "since when did you become the authority on this process," then you should have a sense of what a process authority is. Quite simply, these are certified process engineers with many years of experience in consumer products. It's a tight-knit group of specialists, so once you start to meet industry experts, you'll hear about the same players many times. The PAs require various documents, including formulation, process maps, etc. Then, they evaluate the suitability of the process and issue authorization to begin production (for a small fee). The requirements vary by product type. In many product categories, a PAL is legally required by the FDA prior to production. Do some research on your product category. In general, everyone should get a PAL before beginning scale production.
3. ***Food Safety and Food Defense Plans:*** The food safety and defense plans are basic requirements of the GFSI

certification. In order to pass the audit and begin running your product, a food safety plan will need to be developed specifically around your product's hazards. Same thing with the food defense plan, which basically ensure that some crazy person doesn't contaminate your product on purpose. You can find examples of these online and the co-packer should have a template from other clients.

4. *Challenge Study:* These studies are a great way to validate product stability and provide substantiation of process suitability for the process authority. They involve inoculating the product with various organisms and tracking what happens. Typically, they are performed on pathogens and spoilage. The pathogen challenge is related to food safety (i.e. E. coli) and the spoilage challenge is related to product quality (i.e. APC). The pass/fail criteria need to follow a combination of government regulations and product-specific guardrails, so work with the lab conducting the testing to ensure proper parameters are in place.
5. *Commercial Quality Audits:* One of the best decisions I made early in Ritual's lifecycle was to bring in outside consultants to support building the CQS. I had never worked directly in quality and didn't have a chemistry background, so I knew there were capability gaps. I found an ex-colleague from Kraft-Heinz, who had started his own firm. He staffed a beverage expert from Pepsi with 40+ years of experience on my project. I brought them in for an audit of my contract manufacturer and continued to work with their firm for the duration of Ritual's existence as an independent company. After the audit, they provided a detailed punch list of mission critical projects. Incorporate

the cost of these audits into your budget. It was absolutely critical to Ritual's quality journey. For reference, the firm is called ***Commercial Quality and Food Safety Solutions*** (https://cqafss.com/).

6. ***Certificate of Analysis (CoA):*** Lastly, establish programs with your suppliers to validate quality of the incoming raw materials. The CoA will confirm test results across the key parameters of that product (i.e. a CoA on flavor extracts might specify APC<1 cpu/mL, meaning the product was tested and cleared for micro prior to shipment).

MANUFACTURING STANDARDS

We will spend a significant amount of time talking about co-packers in pillar four. It is worth mentioning a couple of the key points here related to quality. Work closely with the co-packer to review and refine documentation and ensure they have the proper equipment and utilities to meet your quality specifications:

1. ***Documentation:*** In addition to developing the food safety and defense plans, the co-packer should have detailed processes and documentation relating to GMPs, CIP/COP, and corrective actions. GMPs are good manufacturing practices and should specify how they will keep their facility clean and sterile. CIP and COP are clean in place /clean out of place; these involve sterilization and sanitation of the equipment during changeovers between products or in regular intervals. It is very important to align on the CIP/COP frequency before your product is produced. These should be conducted at each changeover of product

SKU and, depending on product sensitivity, they should be conducted every 24-48 hours. Work with the process authority to develop the needs for your product and ensure the co-packer is aligned to complete those CIPs according to this regular cadence. Additionally, they should have an effective process for conducting root cause analyses and building corrective actions. I've worked with several co-packers in my career that had no processes for finding root causes of recurring problems. I found myself conducting those RCA's on their behalf, which is very difficult to do when you're working with third-party employees who don't report to you.

2. ***Equipment and Utilities***: Depending on the product type, it may require treatment to achieve quality standards. For liquid, a good example is pasteurization or hot fill. Liquid products with a pH between 3.0-4.6 often require a kill step including heat. Some products can be filled hot, which is the gold standard. Hot fill involves heating the product to high temperatures and filling, which sanitizes the bottle and cap (i.e. this is how sports drinks are processed). Another possibility is tunnel pasteurization, which is typically done with aluminum cans (beer, all the sparkling water beverages, etc.). This involves filling the cans at room temperature, then passing through a hot tunnel to sterilize (also gold standard). Other products may need to be filled cold or at room temperature. These products can be flash pasteurized in a process called HTST (high temperature, short time). Either way, find a co-packer who has the equipment and experience with these processes. This requirement can be a significant challenge and source of cap-ex requirements. Lastly, ensure sufficient utilities are in place. An example

would be the water system. Validate they have an appropriate RO (reverse osmosis) water system and run studies on the water to ensure it is properly sanitizing the incoming city water. Additionally, review boilers, chillers, and other utilities to confirm they can support process requirements.

3-C. The Wrap: Quick Facts for Benchmarks

Much is made of startup failure rates. As noted earlier, about 90% of startups fail to survive in the long-run, and about 50% fail to survive five years (see QR below). They fail for myriad reasons, with the top culprits including poor market fit, bad marketing strategies, and cash flow issues. The point being, it is incredibly difficult to find a space to play within existing product categories or create your own category. Even if you've found a market niche, it's really hard to create a product that can succeed. Finally, if you've been fortunate enough to find the right market and build a great product, it can still be difficult to navigate market constraints and effectively manage cash flow. If all those boxes have been checked, you better make damn sure it's not the operations team that blows up the business! Failure to develop a robust, commercially scalable quality system is a surefire way to destroy any business.

Follow these steps outlined and customize them to meet product attributes/vulnerabilities. Leverage industry experts to provide the kind of consulting that is actually useful (assisting with your operating manual, connecting with process authorities, developing the specifications, etc.). Don't allow your business to become another statistic. Put your effort, energy, and capital into developing a best-in-class CQS.

Here are a few benchmarks. Note: this entire section is very difficult to write broadly. Take this one with a grain of salt. I'll provide some numbers in the beverage industry, but these will be different in food. It should give you an idea of the factors you will need to develop for your product.

Factor	Benchmark
Product hold times	In beverages, blended batches should be pasteurized within 24 hours and filled within 12 hours of blending.
Label drift	Co-packers should be able to keep the label within +/- 5mm (this is a fairly generous limit; 1 or 2mm would be reasonable).
Micro limits	In beverages, here are some norms (consult your Process Authority): APC<100 cfu/mL Yeast, mold, lactic acid bacteria, acetic acid bacteria <10 cfu/mL
Log reductions	Challenges studies typically require 5 log reductions in pathogen and spoilage testing.
Pasteurization temps	Product in 3.0-4.1 pH range will typically have 175-190 F ranges, with times varying (longer hold times at lower temps, shorter hold times at higher temps). For reference only. As noted, consult your Process Authority.
Shelf life	Beverages will need a minimum of 12 months shelf life, closer to 16-18 months when feeding through distributor networks.

PILLAR 4

MANUFACTURING

4-A. The Situation: Setting the Scene

It's a natural human instinct to care more about the end state than all the work leading up to it. We see this in politics and economics all the time, when people reference downstream statistics like annual GDP growth, trade imbalance, the national debt, unemployment, the CPI (price inflation), and many more. We also see it with companies in annual reporting, product launches, or even demographic discussions. Usually what ensues (whether the numbers are good or bad) is that people respond to these results by locking into one variable, consistent with their pre-existing biases, and proceed to isolate and extrapolate everything else they need to "prove" their original view was always correct. It's amazing to watch how the same piece of data can mean something totally different to a free-market economist versus a democratic socialist. Oftentimes, both parties are oversimplifying a more complex network of inputs and outputs (note: another good reason why you should never isolate and extrapolate everything from one variable in a multi-variate analysis).

When people think about the operations of startup companies in CPG, they tend to focus their attention on manufacturing. It is the main event, where the rubber truly meets the road. However, if you've built the strong foundation outlined in the first three pillars of this section, manufacturing becomes an exercise in execution. I recently read Ben Hogan's ***Five Lessons of Golf***, a 128-page novella on the golf swing. On the third page of the first lesson, I realized my grip has been all wrong for 25 years. A few minor adjustments substantially improved my ball striking. That is how manufacturing works in a nutshell. A few minor mistakes, oversights, or lack of attention to critical details in the fundamentals can have catastrophic consequences in manufacturing.

Many of these fundamentals should already be in place, based on your reliable forecasting & planning, your durable network of material suppliers, and your robust quality program. Now, we'll cover the remaining fundamentals in establishing and building partnerships with dependable manufacturers. We'll discuss how to find them, what to put in a contract, how to hold them accountable, and how to ensure your products are made right the first time, on time, and on budget.

4-B. The Core: Section Contents

- Objective: How to establish and maintain a manufacturing partnership
- Key Components:
    - Identifying and Vetting a Co-Packer
    - Pilot Programs
    - Negotiating the Contract
    - Inventory Accuracy
    - Systems and Communication
    - Champion/Challenger Model
    - Relationship Management

IDENTIFYING AND VETTING A CO-PACKER

When it finally comes time to conduct the first production run, it can feel like an insurmountable challenge. Where can I produce this product? Search engines are typically not all that effective at finding the right match. Think of it like a job interview, because that's effectively the task. Are you better off hopping on *Indeed* and applying for 30 jobs, or reaching out to people in your network to try and find a match? The reality is that a little bit of both is necessary. I'll focus on strategies that might not come to mind immediately.

Finding A Co-Packer Connection

1. *Formula Creator:* As mentioned in the preamble, the assumption here is that we are starting with a core product formulation. In the product profile section, we discussed using a flavor house, innovation hub, etc. to develop the product. These are the best folks to link you with a co-packer. They will understand the base product, the processing constraints, and have historical context on the competence of various co-packers. Start with them and see if they can get you a warm connection.
2. *Packaging Supplier:* A more subtle option is to discuss with your packaging supplier. There are different models within co-packing. Some co-packers provide ***turn-key*** service, which means they purchase the materials from their own suppliers, and the brand pays them for the finished product, including the packaging. As a side note, I would advise against the turn-key option, as the co-packer will be less likely to fiercely negotiate on pass-through materials.

They simply pass on supplier increases to you, the end user. Regardless, this relationship gives packaging suppliers a good sense of available co-packers in different packaging formats that will match the packaging you've selected.

3. *Friends in Big CPG:* Call up any of your friends who work for big CPG companies like Kraft-Heinz, Pepsi, Coca-Cola, Unilever, etc. It's best to find someone in operations or in the innovation team. Don't be miffed by the fact that your product could one day play in the same category. Some people will take your call, and some won't. If a friend of a friend wanted my advice on co-packing, I would take the call.
4. *Private Label Products:* You might be able to reverse engineer the origin of a private-label product. Pick up some products with similar packaging at Target or Costco and check out the back label address line. These typically list where the product is produced. From here, you should be able to search co-packers in the area.

Pre-Screening Potential Co-Packers

After creating a list of potential co-packers, narrow it down to the most attractive options based on a series of KPIs:

1. *Similar Product Offerings:* Ideally, they should run products in similar packaging formats to your product. The packaging format determines the equipment needs, and very few co-packers are willing to drop $100-200K worth of capital on a new brand with no sales.
2. *Geographic Location:* You or someone on your team should be present at every production run for the entire time you work with that co-packer. This might sound

excessive, but you would be shocked how quickly the SOPs developed in the quality section can get tossed aside. Again, no one will care as much about your product as you. The SOPs you develop will be second nature to you, but your co-packer has a booklet full of procedures for every brand they produce. If they run your product quarterly, it's very likely your procedures will be forgotten the week after production. You need to be on-site to remind them each time. Find a location that allows easy travel to the site. Also, look for states with favorable tax policies and effective shipping lanes. This will reduce tolling fees and overall logistics cost (both to be discussed later). As Ron Paul and Milton Friedman both pointed out: "Government spending is the tax. They get you now with direct taxes, or they get you later (with inflation or debt)." So, in high taxation states, even though the co-packer pays the taxes, they pass these on to you through higher tolling fees. Texas is a great spot to produce, as it is centrally located and business-friendly. Ohio and Tennessee offer similar benefits.

3. ***Right-Sized Facilities:*** This one is difficult to decipher during pre-screening. The goal is to get a sense of typical batch sizes and MOQs (minimum order quantities). Try to find a previous client (non-competitor) to gather this information. In general, have a good sense of your target and maximum possible batch sizes to find a right-sized match.
4. ***Historical Record:*** This may seem obvious, but always check out the online reviews of previous clients. This is also a good way to find some people who have worked with the co-packer in the past. People LOVE to discuss their old co-packer and most are happy to jump on a call

to review. Also, you can check the FDA's website here (https://datadashboard.fda.gov/oii/index.htm) to find the audit history of this co-packer. See if they have a history of quality issues or failed audits.

5. ***Certifications:*** GFSI certification was discussed in the quality section. For food, confirm the co-packer has SQF, BRC, etc. Determine which claims are core to the brand and ensure the co-packer is properly certified (i.e. gluten-free, kosher, cruelty free, etc.). Most of these claims come with independent third-party validation. For example, NSF is a company that commonly certifies gluten-free facilities.

Stimulating Mutual Interest

Finding a co-packer isn't exactly like finding a dry cleaner. After compiling and ranking a list of options, you can't just drop off your formula and come back in three days to pick up the product. Co-packers are like less-sophisticated venture capitalists. Their revenues come from limited time horizons, as they often produce brands until those brands become large enough for self-sufficiency. Much like a VC, they must invest in a portfolio of brands, which they believe have the potential for spurts of growth. Then, they can capture as much revenue and profitability as possible, for this fixed period of time. It's a romantic relationship where you're having fun, but you know it isn't forever. Therefore, upon establishing a meeting with target co-packers, it's crucial to present your brand like you're pitching an investor; in many ways, you are. Have this ammunition ready for the first call or in-person meeting:

1. ***Consumer Need:*** We're touching on a few items outside the scope of this playbook, but I'll say a brief word on them because they are crucial. Quick sidebar: When I was in

engineering school at The University of Cincinnati, I had to take a History of Rock 'n' Roll elective (another example of how traditional school sucks: to get a job in manufacturing at L'Oreal, I had to write a synopsis on the downfall of The Doors). It's funny how something can be totally useless, until it provides one insight you use for a lifetime. In an utterly worthless class, the "professor" (picture a 55-year-old, washed out, ex-rocker/stoner, who never quite made it) caught my attention with one line: **"If you want someone to pay attention, tell them a story".** It's very simple, but I never thought about it that way. I've used this framework in every speech, presentation, and creative outlet since (see, I just did it). Deploy this tactic in the first conversation with the co-packer. I watched the Ritual founders do this masterfully with suppliers, sponsors, journalists, and anyone else who would listen. Explain the consumer need and how this solution came to fruition (like the Doc Brown moment in ***Back to the Future*** when he invents the Flux Capacitor).

2. ***Go-to-Market Strategy:*** Expand on taking this novel idea to market. Explain the channel strategy and how you will acquire your first big customers. Feel free to embellish a little bit (without lying) about the contacts who will get your brand in front of the key retailers.
3. ***Market Size and Category Vision:*** Develop a realistic three-year vision on the category potential. Don't just draw a ludicrous hockey stick. Show the bottom-up calculations (discussed in forecasting), so they understand you're not delusional.
4. ***Forecasts:*** Show up with practical, detailed forecasts. A big problem for co-packers is that everyone arrives with

grandiose topline numbers: "We're going to produce one million bottles in year one." Most of them can't stand this, as they've seen this movie too many times (spoiler alert: the protagonist gets taken out before hitting 1M bottles). Mind the balance between ***optimistic confidence*** and ***practical realism***. Build multiple scenarios, starting with the expected plan, then a reduced plan, then an aspirational plan. Anchor the conversation around the reduced plan. Show them the mid-level target is well within reach, but let's plan off the reduced option. Let's ensure the economics are sound on the reduced option. If they are, we know the expected plan is going to be a huge win.

5. ***Volume Thresholds:*** As described, determine the ideal and maximum batch sizes. Make sure the MOQ isn't going to bankrupt your company or saddle you with a bunch of expiring inventory you can't sell on time.
6. ***Production Manuals:*** Bring the production manual and have it ready to present. Bind the thing and make it look professional. A co-packer is always thinking about complexity. Mainly, how difficult is your thing to make. Make it very clear that the process experts know the ins and outs. You will be there to help guide their processing teams on the formulation and adjust on the spot as needed.
7. ***One-Point Lessons:*** I always liked the idea of physically building tools for production teams. Make a label gauge that shows in-spec and out-of-spec label placement or fill height. Bring color chips, like the ones used in painting, to confirm the correct color of your product. Small gestures like this go a long way. One of the co-packer's biggest issues is client ambiguity. They start working with a client who gives them

> vague descriptions of standards, production ensues, and all of a sudden the client isn't happy. What do we do with all this product? Who is financially responsible? Is it in-spec or out-of-spec? These are the scenarios co-packers must avoid. Demonstrating organization, thoroughness, and dedication to standards will impress your co-packer. It also evidences commitment to collaboration. In a way, it feels like you're already working together, so the co-packer no longer needs to weigh the pros and cons of this partnership. The partnership has already started. It's like how ***Seinfeld's*** George Constanza used to leave something at a woman's apartment on purpose after a mediocre date. When he returned to retrieve his keys, that's date number two (one more and we've got a relationship)!

Identifying, vetting, and solidifying a co-packer is a lengthy and challenging courtship. Following the preceding steps will guide an objective analysis of the co-packer's proficiency. One other element to layer into the assessment is much more subjective. When you walk the plant, ask yourself whether you want your product produced in that facility. Is it clean and organized, or is there trash all over the floor? Do the workers look engaged and seem friendly, or are they counting the minutes until punch-out time? When you ask people questions, do you get quality answers or find yourself with three more questions? There was a scene in ***Gladiator*** when Maximus exclaims, "Marcus Aurelius had a vision for Rome, and this is NOT it." I've visited subpar places where I found myself having a Maximus moment. You have the KPIs built out and that should do the bulk of the work. However, in the end, if it doesn't pass the sniff test, pull the plug and keep searching.

PILOT PRODUCTION

A new co-packer is a "try before you buy" type of relationship. After landing on a general agreement for partnership, it's crucial to conduct a pilot production run. The goal of this production run is pretty simple: validate they aren't completely full of shit! The co-packer will have boasted about the robust quality controls, their experienced team of experts, and their highly efficient production lines. Go see all these components in action.

Pilot Production Keys

1. ***Pre-Production Preparation***: Ensure they execute the standard pre-production processes detailed in your production manual. This will involve CIP of the equipment (batching and filling). It involves completing a startup checklist, which includes quality checks to ensure the line is clean. They typically use a device called an ATP meter, which requires swabbing the production line, filler, and tanks to ensure no microbiological activity (i.e. no bacteria present). Observe how they conduct this process. How many swabs are they taking? Are they swabbing the correct areas? Have they properly flushed out the old product? Did they clear the line of old packaging materials from previous runs?
2. ***Batch Size:*** Run the smallest batch possible to provide the data needed. This typically involves witnessing "steady-state" production. The first hour of production is usually a wash of startup tweaks and shaking off rust. I would suggest a three-hour minimum of production. For a beverage, consider 1,000 gallons of product to see this in action.

3. ***Product Tolerance:*** Ensure they can achieve and maintain the product specifications. Some key areas to review are fill volume, weight, height, and secondary packaging placement (i.e. labels). Fill heights can drift if a bottle filler isn't properly maintained or is outdated. Labels can be misoriented, drift high or low on the package, or bubble if not placed perfectly. Keep a close eye on these items because, if present more than a couple of times in a few hours of running, imagine what a full week of production will yield.
4. ***Throughput:*** Monitor line speeds and OEE (overall equipment effectiveness—essentially, of the three production hours, how much time is the line consistently running versus stopped). In the early stages, ***overall capacity*** shouldn't be a major concern, but ***excess capacity*** will be crucial (effectively, how much time do they have to run your product). Ensure the co-packer can quickly turn around a PO (purchase order) and meet the requirements on quality, on budget, and on time.
5. ***Post-Production Evaluation***: This final, most critical step, involves a trip back to the commercial quality manual. Conduct all the standard tests, both analytical and sensory. For such a small run with all this attention, they should be able to beat the typical standards. For example, if the APC target is set <100 cfu/mL (reminder: aerobic plate count, micro-organism presence), all samples really should register <1 cfu/mL for the pilot test. It's the ***Butterfly Effect***: small, localized issues become huge issues upon expansion. If micro issues are present in small batches, they will likely be more pronounced in conventional batch sizes.

6. ***Sellable Product***: I recommend selling the product from this batch. You should treat it as a standard production run, only with a lot more eyes on it. There's no reason not to sell this product in the market. In the early days, cash is your bloodline, so don't waste it on overly conservative decision-making. Big companies typically throw away their pilot production inventory. Thomas Sowell describes this type of activity as ***diseconomies of scale***. It's when the company becomes so large that it creates perverse incentives, which are counter-productive to the overall business (i.e. for any one quality manager, it's not worth the risk of releasing a trial batch, even though we know the product is safe and on target—the incremental risk of losing his/her job outweighs the cost of the production, possibly in the $10-40K range).

If all goes well with the pilot production run, it's time to lock in this relationship and make it official. This requires building, negotiating, and signing a manufacturing agreement.

MANUFACTURING AGREEMENT

The manufacturing agreement is probably the third most important contract signed by an early-stage company (#1 being the financing terms with investors and #2 being the founders' agreement). It's important to be precise and practical. I have the same advice here as the procurement section: engage a lawyer to draft it up, but be heavily involved and understand what each section is trying to accomplish. Here are the guts of a solid manufacturing agreement:

Manufacturing Agreement Keys

1. *Relationship Parameters*: Outline the responsibilities of each party at a high level. As described above, co-packers typically work on conversion or turn-key models. Conversion means the brand buys all the materials and the co-packer is responsible for converting them into raw materials. The brand pays a tolling fee for blending, baking, packing, etc. Turn-key involves handing over specs and having the co-packer procure and store materials, in addition to the conversion work (all-inclusive model). I prefer the conversion model because I have confidence in my ability to accurately forecast materials and negotiate the best material price. If the co-packer has a lot of scale and buys similar containers for other clients, perhaps they can exert some power and reduce costs. Gauge this one on your specific circumstances but get it in the contract. Also, discuss exclusivity and add that here. Some co-packers will want exclusive rights to produce your product. Obviously, push back on this if you can (discussed further in the Champion/Challenger section).
2. *Facility*: Highlight specifics around facility management. Talk about what needs to be maintained in the facility (cleanliness, certifications, production and sanitation records). Discuss the minimum equipment standards and how equipment upgrades will be financed. One of the real challenges of being an early-stage brand is getting the co-packer to invest in equipment specifically for your brand. I don't have a silver bullet solution here. I had the best luck starting with semi-automated facilities. Think production

lines with a lot of manual operators but the ability to add modular equipment as you grow. A big mistake (that I made) is attempting to finance a highly automated line before the volume dictates this need. I'm a huge believer in automation and productivity projects, but it's important to scale a facility deliberately.

3. ***Quality:*** No surprise here. Reference the quality manual, which will need to be attached as a supplemental document. Also discuss quality testing. Specifically, will it be conducted in-house or through a third-party lab? Who pays if it is outsourced? I highly recommend outsourcing the testing and covering the costs. There are some obvious problems associated with co-packer-led testing. It's kind of like having the FBI investigate themselves for wrongdoing, as is often done. Not surprisingly, they almost always come back with no evidence of criminal wrongdoing! Use an independent lab to provide a neutral product evaluation. This also helps any disputes, like a form of arbitration. Include recall procedures in this program. What triggers a recall? How does financial responsibility work? Recalls can destroy an early-stage company very quickly, not just because of the reputational damage, but also from the astronomical costs that can rapidly accumulate. Lay it out in a manner that articulates which party will pay for the recall.
4. ***Orders, Pricing and Invoicing***: This takes us back to the negotiation section of the procurement pillar. Outline details on placing a production order. How far in advance are forecasts needed and when do the POs need to be placed? A good general rule is to provide a rolling 12-month forecast, updated monthly. Issue formal POs around

two months before production needs to be completed. Typically, I provide an annual forecast in November for the next year. Then, I issue a PO in November for January production and so forth. This is dependent on factors like shelf-life, which dictate the production frequency (discussed in the supply planning section). Include a section with tiered pricing. I really like the use of volume discounts and rebates in the manufacturing agreement. Invoicing can also be used as a tool by adding discounts for pre-payment or early payment on 30–60 day terms. For example, net 30—a typical co-packer arrangement—means you need to pay them within 30 days of receiving the invoice. I like to include "2% 10, net 30" terms, which means I receive a 2% discount if I pay within 10 days of receiving the invoice. It should be closer to 3-5% off if you pay 2-4 weeks before production. All co-packers are different. Some require payment at the time of the PO. You should be compensated for that added risk in the form of lower tolling fees. Include all these details in a series of clear charts, as you will likely need to reference this information in the future. Also, get a sense of the co-packer's financial status. If they say "we've been pretty slow lately," hold off the pre-payments. It would be disastrous to send in a pre-payment a month before the co-packer goes bankrupt and never receive your product.

5. ***Term and Termination***: Develop contract duration and what needs to happen to end the relationship. I like 2–3-year terms with annual price reviews. As your company continues to grow, capture some volume-based savings. Make sure to include an outlet if things aren't working out with the co-packer. I try to avoid minimum production

quantities because there is too much volatility in the early stages to lock in volume commitments. This is where volume tiers are particularly useful.

6. *Liability*: Include language around liability for specific types of events, like the recall situation I mentioned earlier. Also discuss the case of non-conforming products, which will need to be destroyed. Who covers the cost of destruction, labor, and all the material costs? Think through all the things that can go wrong (a good exercise to do anyways as part of a risk assessment) and discuss it with your co-packer. Highlight the specific events with the highest probability of occurrence.
7. *Transfer of Goods*: Finally, detail how the ownership of the goods will be transferred. How will the product be physically moved from the co-packer to your distribution centers or customers? When does your company take ownership of the product, and thus, liability of the material? Typically, you will take ownership when the product leaves the production facility. This is why it is a good idea to get a ***stock-throughput*** insurance policy. It covers the materials on the road and in your warehouses at the distribution centers.

Hopefully that's enough contract talk for you. I went into a lot of detail on these items because they are key to maintaining a healthy relationship with the co-packer. Contracts typically seem like administrative, check the box activities. The manufacturing agreement is different. Note that I mentioned several times to discuss these items with your co-packer. Don't just send them the form to add red lines. The goal is to engage in a dialogue now to avoid very difficult conversations in the future. It's like a prenuptial agreement; a little uncomfortable to discuss upfront, but very useful if future issues arise.

INVENTORY MANAGEMENT

Another sexy Ops topic is inventory management. At this point in the project, you can tell I'm an avid defender of free market capitalism. However, I've often said if a socialist was trying to convert me, a compelling pitch would be the offer of "no more inventory management." There's no need for cost accounting, so nothing matters. I don't have to track down 2,500 missing caps after all. Okay, I'm listening. I jest, but the reason inventory management is so painful is because there's so much money on the line. A miscalculation here or a misplaced pallet there and $30,000 worth of product can be gone forever. Again, in the early stages, this is significant enough to bankrupt a company. This is why you must develop a comprehensive system to account for inventory. Here are my recommendations for improved inventory management:

Inventory Management Keys

1. *Inventory Management System*: As mentioned in section 1-B, an ERP system is crucial, even in the early stages (note: an inventory management system is embedded in the ERP). I recently participated in a mentor session with a young entrepreneur who was struggling with inventory problems. She was having a hard time converting single units into the sellable multipack. I was a bit confused and asked her how she had it set up in the inventory management system. She

responded that they didn't have an inventory management system. Well, now I get it! This is an example of how a very simple, standard task can become very complicated without the help of one of these systems. As I mentioned, I used Cin 7 Core, which was relatively affordable and reliable. You should be able to find many options that fit your budget, since one avoided mistake could pay for the whole system.

2. ***Accounting Support***: Another big advantage was the use of an external accounting firm. We used them to do all the basic accounting, convert our raw materials into finished goods in our inventory system, and complete all basic inbound and outbound transactions. It's more costly but it's definitely worth the expense. We used Accountfully and they did an excellent job at an affordable rate. Offshoring this function for simpler, data intensive activities is possible, which should lower the cost. As mentioned in the RFP section, I worked with a team of folks in Indonesia, which I recommend: (https://dpoandco.com/bpo).
3. ***Shared Documents for Inbound Receipt***: Implement a basic shared spreadsheet with your software of choice and get the co-packer to begin using that document. They will log inbound receipts of materials to confirm material accuracy (see Figure 11). This is a procedure for early-stage startups. Ideally, you would be using an integrated system, like SAP, and the manufacturer will have a portal to enter the data, scan pallet tickets, etc. This is typical later in the process, so I wanted to explain what you will do in the early days. Also, reference the ***Inventory Management*** sheet in the supplemental materials.

4. *Post-Production Recap*: Create a tab in the shared spreadsheet for post-production recap. Back to the previous section, send POs to the manufacturer a month or two in advance of the production run. These POs specify the target quantities of each SKU. However, in an actual production run, the finished quantities will vary (should be no more than +/-5% and should usually be less than the target, due to some product waste). The post-production recap will confirm the exact quantities produced at the end of the run, so you can convert the exact quantities of materials into finished goods (see Figure 12).
5. *Remaining Material Count*: Add one more tab to your shared spreadsheet for remaining material. There will be some scrap of packaging and raw materials (again, if it exceeds +/-5% there's a production problem). Adding a maximum scrap factor to your manufacturing agreement is also a good idea. After production, have the co-packer count the remaining materials and add them to the spreadsheet (see Figure 13).
6. *Conversion Exercise with Scrap*: After production, have the accounting firm convert the raw and packaging materials into finished goods in the ERP. They will complete the basic transactions to confirm what was consumed versus scrapped in the production environment. Make all those adjustments before the next production run of that SKU. Typically, if I need multiple batches of the same SKU, I run the batches consecutively and make the adjustments after production. The co-packer will appreciate this and it simplifies the inventory management.

7. ***Inventory Locations:*** We will discuss distribution centers in more detail in the next section. Just be aware that some brands use the co-packer as the distribution center, while others work with a 3PL. I strongly recommend using a 3PL as early in the process as possible. It's one extra touchpoint and comes with additional cost, but they will do a substantially better job of managing the finished product than a co-packer. This is for all the same reasons I recommend using the third-party quality lab. It's best to bring in material just-in-time for production, convert it into finished goods, and ship it out of the facility (after passing quality testing).

		This column entered by co-packer upon receipt		
Ingredient/Packaging	**Scheduled Qty**	**Delivered Qty**	**Variance**	**Units**
RM_Erythritol	50	50	0	lbs.
RM_Citric Acid	50	50	0	lbs.
RM_Vitamin and Plant Extract	55	55	0	Gal
RM_Fruit Punch Flavor	110	100	-10	Gal
RM_Sodium Benzoate	50	50	0	lbs.
PKG_16z Bottle	150,000	150,000	0	each
PKG_Cap	150,000	150,000	0	each
PKG_Label	200,000	180,000	-20,000	each
PKG_12pk Case	15,000	15,000	0	each

Figure 11. Material Receipt

This section is similar to the modeling section, so open the supplemental materials and start playing with your company's data.

Production Date	FG Item	Item Code	Scheduled Qty	Delivered Qty	Variance	% Variance	Lot Code	Quality Tests approved	ERP assembly #	Invoice #	Invoice Paid
2026-01-04	FG-16z Fruit Punch 12pk	10001	400	380	-20	-5%	MAN26004LN2 001	YES	FG-23249	INV-2421	NO
2026-01-05	FG-16z Fruit Punch 12pk	10001	400	390	-10	-3%	MAN26005LN2 002	YES	FG-23250	INV-2421	NO
2026-01-06	FG-16z Fruit Punch 12pk	10001	400	380	-20	-5%	MAN26006LN2 003	YES	FG-23251	INV-2421	NO
2026-01-07	FG-16z Grape 12pk	10002	500	480	-20	-4%	MAN26007LN2 001	YES	FG-23252	INV-2421	NO
2026-01-08	FG-16z Grape 12pk	10002	500	490	-10	-2%	MAN26008LN2 002	YES	FG-23253	INV-2421	NO
2026-01-11	FG-16z Pimento Punch 12pk	10003	150	145	-5	-3%	MAN26011LN2 001	NO	FG-23254	INV-2421	NO

Figure 12. Post-Production Recap

	This column entered by co-packer upon completing production					
Ingredient/Packaging	**Post-production remaining Qty**	**ERP calculated remaining Qty**	**Variance**	**Units**	**Variance %**	**Status**
RM_Erythritol	4.98	5.00	-0.02	lbs.	0%	within scrap factor; adjust ERP
RM_Citric Acid	7.75	8.00	-0.25	lbs.	-3%	within scrap factor; adjust ERP
RM_Vitamin and Plant Extract	11.80	12.00	-0.20	Gal	-2%	within scrap factor; adjust ERP
RM_Fruit Punch Flavor	29.00	30.00	-1.00	Gal	-3%	within scrap factor; adjust ERP
RM_Sodium Benzoate	4.80	5.00	-0.20	lbs.	-4%	within scrap factor; adjust ERP
PKG_16z Bottle	18,800.00	20,000.00	-1,200.00	each	-6%	exceeds scrap; investigate
PKG_Cap	19,800.00	20,000.00	-200.00	each	-1%	within scrap factor; adjust ERP
PKG_Label	18,000.00	25,000.00	-7,000.00	each	-28%	exceeds scrap; investigate
PKG_12pk Case	1,986.00	2,000.00	-14.00	each	-1%	within scrap factor; adjust ERP

Figure 13. Remaining Inventory

SYSTEMS AND COMMUNCATION

Another spoiler alert: most co-packers aren't at the cutting edge of the AI revolution. We just detailed the challenges and ramifications of inventory management issues. There are several other transactions that will need to be initiated in the ERP system and transferred to the co-packer's systems and vice versa.

The main activities are placing POs for future production, paying invoices for past production, transferring quality and operational documentation, and all the inventory management data previously discussed. This is an inherently difficult process for most early-stage startups. The ideal arrangement is an integrated system with a manufacturer portal. For example, if your company is on SAP, there are external modules that can integrate at the co-packer's site. This enables seamless exchange of information. Most of the time, this level of technical sophistication does not exist at a co-packer. The alternative is to utilize shared sheets in Microsoft (my recommendation), Google, Dropbox, or whatever you prefer. During the scoping phase, ask the co-packer what they use for the management of these workflows. Have them demo a transfer of information. Basically, confirm the system actually works. While it's uncommon for co-packers to have a very sophisticated IT system, it is very common for them to insist that they have the latest technology and seamless integration.

One of the real keys to managing this information is personal touch. As we started to grow, I was incredibly fortunate to hire two excellent employees: one for supply chain management and one for quality. My supply chain manager had weekly calls with our co-packer and distributor, which were critical for maintaining accurate, reliable information. My quality manager was on-site for every production run and became an extension of the co-packer's team. They would often ask him for directions on operating procedures. This is the type of evolution you want to see with the co-packer. It's easy to say "we're in this together," but much harder to demonstrate in practice. Being present on the site and relentless in capturing real-time information demonstrates commitment to the partnership and attention to detail.

CHAMPION/CHALLENGER MODEL

As you can probably see from the length of this section, a tremendous amount of work is required to build and maintain a co-packer relationship. Encountering a system with this many requirements usually means a lot can wrong. For an early-stage consumer product company, a co-packer relationship turned sour can put you out of business. You're probably wondering how many of these "can put you out of business" references I'm going to make, but it's true and you need to understand that from the beginning.

For this reason, I've always preferred a network of two co-packers. We call it the Champion/Challenger model. Typically, this isn't possible in year one. However, if you have a successful start to the enterprise and are showing signs of rapid growth, years 2-3 are a good time to start re-enforcing the production network. Follow all the steps in the first section and find an alternate co-packer. The are many trade-offs to consider during that evaluation. It provides an opportunity to diversify geographically. On the other side of that coin, if you pick a nearby co-packer, it makes materials management much easier (i.e. send the materials to one site and limit the amount of on-hand inventory). This reduces freight and complexity. It also allows site visits to both co-packers in one trip (or visit both sites often if you live nearby). I recommend the local approach at the beginning. Reduce the complexity, cost, and travel. After continued growth, it might make sense to re-consider geographic diversification.

Additionally, you'll need to consider how to split the volume. Try to land on a 75/25 volume split (75% with your Champion co-packer, 25% with your Challenger). A good way to achieve this is to dedicate one SKU to the Challenger. Again, this greatly reduces complexity and minimizes the chance of inconsistencies. Product consistency is a key consideration upon commissioning the second co-packer. When I first initiated this change at Ritual, I remember how subtle differences had a huge impact on the finished product. We noticed the pH on the RO (reverse osmosis) water was different between the two sites. This had an impact on finished product pH, which would impact taste profile and adherence to product specifications. It required slightly different procedures at each plant to land on identical taste profiles. This added complexity puts additional strain on a startup operator's most precious resource: time (maybe second most important to your cash). Ultimately, I felt the resource costs were well worth the benefits of supply risk mitigation and increased negotiation power.

RELATIONSHIP SUSTAINABILTY

Sustainability in the Start-Ops leader's network is absolutely crucial and extends far beyond reducing waste. It's about building a durable system that can grow as the business grows. The relationship with the co-packer is at the core of a sustainable operating model. So, here's a quick recap on the keys to a long-lasting and productive co-packer relationship:

Relationship Management Keys

1. ***Quality Management:*** Quality issues are the quickest and most surefire way for a relationship to dissolve. This is why developing the quality program previously discussed and testing it through the pilot program is so critical. It's also why a detailed, specific manufacturing agreement must be developed upfront. I think this is the most uncomfortable part of the pre-production relationship, but it must be done. A quality issue will arise. Manufacturing is just plain hard, so be prepared for the what if scenarios.
2. ***Timely Payment:*** We spoke in the procurement section about prompt payments. Multiply that by 100 with the co-packer. They operate on very slim margins with long-term success hurdles. Make sure they are paid on time and in full.
3. ***Accurate Forecasting:*** Co-packers deal with a very transient workforce. Typically, they have standard safety factors for planning personnel (i.e. if they need 30 operators that day, they schedule 35, planning for a few to not show up). They are also very tight on cash and need to deploy capital for frequent plant upgrades and maintenance. Make their lives easier by executing the production commitments. Be communicative along the way. Let them know when you see downturns and need to reduce or push out production. Don't wait until the last minute, when they've already planned the labor, to pull the plug or move things around.
4. ***On-Time Material Delivery:*** Ensure the packaging and raw materials are on site and ready to go, per the SOPs. Usually, the material should arrive 1-2 weeks before production. Make sure this is the case so they have time to count, inspect, and get setup for production.

5. ***Open Discussion of Problems:*** I can't over-emphasize the importance of being present at the site. Keep your eyes open and make a list of items that don't make sense to you. If you see a hose that might touch product laying in a puddle of water, ask for clarification. If you see an operator doing something unsafe, mention it to your point of contact. Don't assume everything is fine. Most of the time, it probably isn't. The more upfront you are as issues arise, the less chance these items will accumulate into a much larger problem. I struggled with this at first. I would accumulate a large list of issues (10-15) and discuss them all at once. Maybe one or two would get addressed but the rest remained. Dig in early and often.
6. ***Backup Supplier Acknowledgment:*** When planning to activate the champion/challenger model, find the right time and communicate this to the primary co-packer. Tell them they are the primary and volumes will continue to grow, as they have for the last one to two years. Then, explain the need for the second co-packer. Maybe it's for a better geographical footprint. Maybe you fear their plant might get hit by a tornado. Overall, be honest and transparent.

4-C. The Wrap: Quick Facts for Benchmarks

Is your head spinning? It probably should be. Co-packer collaboration is certainly not easy. But look at the bright side: it's a very exciting component of the overall process and is actually a lot of fun. All the hard work put into designing the product, raising money, building programs, selling it in, forecasting and planning, and developing a commercial quality system, finally comes to life. As hard as this program is, it will all be worth it when the product starts rolling off the production lines.

A key point to remember is that you can't have it all when working with a co-packer. I remember seeing a discussion with Jordan Peterson at Oxford. He was discussing speech laws with one of the students, who was advocating for the implementation of laws to police speech, because of concerns about the downside of allowing people to attack others online. I thought Peterson brilliantly illuminated the obvious problem with this type of thinking. He pointed out that often times, a problem exists, and people float a solution. Then, they assume that all other conditions remain the same, only the problem is eliminated. Peterson said "No! That's not how it works." The reality is, in most cases, your solution comes with a cost. The true test is to evaluate if the benefit from the regulation is worth the cost. In this case, does having the government policing what's in and out of bounds for online memes create a better or worse society overall?

This is exactly how managing a co-packer works. You are going to want a suite of services from them. You'll want them to have plenty of capacity to run the product and flexibility to accept purchase orders on very short notice. You'll want superior quality on every batch, but you'll also want adherence to plan, ensuring the product is delivered on-time. You'll want a level of malleability, such that new products in new formats can be produced. You'll want them to have the vision to outlay the capital expenditures to produce with best-in-class technology. You'll want a co-packer who takes responsibility for errors and covers the cost of production mistakes. And you'll also want a friendly partner, with a solution-oriented attitude. Let me be clear, until the UCI (Utopian Co-packer Institute) launches, you're going to have a hard time finding all these benefits. As mentioned in this section, prioritize quality and on-time delivery. Ensure the robust manufacturing agreement is in place, clearly outlining financial responsibilities in various scenarios. Here are a few benchmarks:

Factor	Benchmark
Lead time for Pos	This refers to how quickly you can get into production. A standard number is about 2 months (i.e. I send a purchase order January 1 to start production the first week of March).
Annual commitments	You should be able to operate without a fixed volume commitment per facility. If they want to include this in the contract, try to add a % of your total production instead of a nominal number (I.e. 75% of our annual production will be produced here instead of 500K bottles).
Minimum order qty's (MOQs)	In beverages, this is usually by the batch. You should be able to produce as small as 1K gallon batches. For other product types, cover this as a key point in your checklist for vetting co-packers.
Payment terms	This can also vary. I've had co-packers who wanted the money upfront, those who wanted it 50% down, 50% after production, and standard 30-day payment terms. Use this as a key negotiation point in the contract.
Line speeds	Slower speed bottling lines (ideal for early-stage, small volumes) will run around 40-60 BPM (bottles per min). You will reach 80-100 BPMs as volumes climb. Again, with other product formats, this is a key question in the vetting process. Faster isn't always better. Gauge the combination of speed and OEE.
OEE (overall equipment effectiveness)	This measures how often the line is running when it's supposed to be running. It should be between 60-75%.
Tank sizes	For beverages, there should be a variety of tank sizes ranging between 500-6,000 gallons. These get larger as volumes increase. Same caveat on other product lines: this is a key criterion during the vetting process

PILLAR 5

DISTRIBUTION

5-A. The Situation: Setting the Scene

Fitness is a core component of my lifestyle, and I believe it makes me more effective in the workplace. One of the many similarities between fitness and operations is the linear progression of a good workout. I segment mine into a warmup, main event, abs, and cool down stretch. I follow this pattern with virtually every workout. However, I've probably only followed this sequence since I was in my mid-thirties. I often think about how much time I wasted doing curls and bench press in my twenties. The easiest part of the program to compromise is the final cooldown. We all can make a million excuses, notably, I need to get to work. But if you skip the cool down and stretch, the muscles don't receive the proper recovery mechanism and are not going to grow to the same extent. You can do everything right for 90% of the workout but the whole thing can be wasted by skipping a deliberate finish. That's how logistics works within an overall supply chain. We traveled through four extensive, foundational pillars. You planned correctly to meet demand. You bought the right materials at the right price. You built a meticulous quality manual to make the product right the first time and every time. Finally, the product rolled off the production line according to plan. Now, it's time to ensure that you don't screw it up in the last mile. Let's discuss how to build the distribution network, how to ensure reliability in order management, and how to get the product from point A to B.

5-B. The Core: Section Contents

- Objective: How to design and build a distribution network
- Key Components:
    - 3PL Requirements
    - Designing the Network
    - Wholesale Norms
    - Direct-to-Consumer
    - Order Management

3PL REQUIREMENTS

We completed Ritual's first large production runs in the beginning of 2020. At the time, we worked with a contract manufacturer that had a huge property with a massive warehousing capacity. It made a lot of sense to keep everything on site. We stored our raw and packaging materials on site, along with all our finished goods. They prepped and shipped our orders to customers. They even supported our ecommerce business with kitting and prep work. It was a simple, centralized system, and I was fairly content with it... right up until we started reconciling inventory. Most co-packers are good at blending product and putting it in a package. Managing orders and inventory can often be a different story. Every quarter, I would ask them to count our finished goods and compare that count to the reports in my inventory management system. Without fail, every count was between 10-20% off from my numbers, and always in one direction (i.e. my inventory system said we should have more pallets in the warehouse than we did). I spent countless hours working with them to resolve these issues, to no avail. Our ecommerce prep was often behind schedule and not very flexible. Additionally, we had a couple of shipment issues where the wrong pallets went to customers. In one case, our best customer was shipped a test pallet of product, which was supposed to be destroyed. The bottles didn't even have labels!

At that point, I decided to move our product into an external third-party logistics firm (3PL). This was one of the best decisions I made in Ritual's early stages. In general, that third-party separation keeps everything copacetic. They provide a timely, reliable count of finished goods after every production run. This verification is crucial to ensure the production numbers listed in the production log were precisely met. It also provides useful separation in case of any future disputes with the co-packer. I recall another scenario when we had a dispute about a quality issue. I was holding payment for the production until we completed a root cause analysis and had a true understanding of culpability. Seems reasonable, right? Well, I was told by the co-packer that until I submitted that payment, they would not be processing any outstanding customer shipments (i.e. they held the product hostage and threatened our business continuity).

For these reasons, I highly recommend bringing in a 3PL early in the process. There are several KPIs you should use when qualifying the effectiveness of your 3PL:

3PL KPIs

1. *CFR (Case Fill Rate)*: What % of orders are shipped/picked up on time. This should be in the high 90% range (97-99%) for an early-stage company.
2. *Order Accuracy:* Measures that the right SKUs and quantities arrived to the correct customer. It should be 99.5% or higher.
3. *Inventory Accuracy:* This is a big one. Upon completing month-end financial close or full-physical inventories, the

inventory management system should tie out with the physical product. This should be something like 99.5% accurate. I harp on this subject a lot because it's really easy to screw this up and be stuck with product write-offs. These write-offs are especially pernicious when you don't have the cash to waste.

4. ***Special Case Flexibility:*** Not a typical KPI per se, but you should be able to gauge how reactive your 3PL is to a rapidly changing business. For example, ecommerce can be highly seasonal and volatile. A ***Real Housewife of New Jersey*** named Bethanny Frankel posted a video on Instagram of her drinking Ritual and our sales shot up 300% overnight. The 3PL needs to be able to respond to this type of situation and get the new orders out the door quickly.

These KPIs are in addition to all the usual aspects like capacity and cost. We'll dive into the typical components of cost in more detail in the subsequent sections.

NETWORK DESIGN

If I've convinced you to use a 3PL, several questions will probably arise. Where do I find one? How many different distribution centers are needed and where should they be located? What type of services should be conducted in each facility? This will vary dramatically by business. Here are a few considerations when designing the network:

Design Considerations

1. ***Route-to-Market:*** The first thing you need to do is understand your route-to-market and customer base. Route-to-

market is a fancy way of saying the channel and distribution strategy. What % of the business utilizes B2B wholesale sales versus D2C (direct to consumer) ecommerce sales? Do you use a distributor or sell direct to the retailers? Generally speaking, the more wholesale business as a % of your total volume, the more concentrated your network of distribution centers can be.

2. ***Product Parameters***: You'll also need to understand how the product's specific features impact the network. How long is your product shelf life? The shorter shelf-life items might mean you need more distribution nodes. More nodes mean shorter delivery times, which might be critical, depending on the product. Additionally, how urgently do your customers need your product? Is it the type of item ordered last minute with next-day delivery requirements or is it a recurring item they purchase monthly and can wait a couple of days for arrival? Think through these parameters when designing the network.
3. ***Optimal Simplicity***: As we've discussed, when you are first starting up, simplicity is key. You will have limited support resources for the first couple of years (if any). Think about how to move product, raw, and packaging materials through this network. Remember, you need to forecast quantities for each material at each site. Because of this, limit how many materials are housed within each site.

Network Options

The are several different ways to configure your network. They boil down to one of three distinct categories: centralized, regional, and hub and spoke models. See figure 14 for the visual and let's discuss which type is appropriate for your business:

1. ***Centralized model:*** this involves moving all your materials to one centralized distribution center (DC). This typically works well for very early-stage companies (years 1-2) and products that aren't needed in a rush. It greatly simplifies managing materials, planning inventory, and enacting SOPs, since it's only one facility to commission. The central model ties up the least amount of cash, since you don't need to spread inventory through multiple facilities. The downside includes longer lead times and higher delivery costs, as you need to ship your product across multiple UPS/FedEx shipping zones.
2. ***Regional model:*** this model entails activating 2-4 different DCs with the same 3PL. Side note: I have met some entrepreneurs who use different 3PLs across a regional network. I highly discourage this approach, as it creates more complexity and headaches for you; the last thing you need, is headaches. In this model, you'll typically have an East coast DC, a West coast DC, and 1-2 DC's in the Midwest. Ohio is a common Midwest location (usually Columbus) because the highway network creates easy access to the SE region, including FL. This model adds complexity to managing inventory but reduces delivery costs and lead times. It's better for a slightly more mature startup (years 3-5) with significant national customer coverage.
3. ***Hub and Spoke:*** this model is a hybrid of the centralized and regional models. It involves sending product to a centralized hub, where the 3PL forwards the materials to several regional fulfillment centers. This can range from 5-20 different DCs. Examples of this type of 3PL include ShipBob, ShipMonk, and Deliverr (acquired by Flexport). This model is ideal for a business heavily weighted towards eCommerce (>60% of your volume).

To summarize:

Type	Pros	Cons	Suited for
Centralized	• Lower inventory holding costs • Less complexity • Easier for planning • Less training required	• Longer delivery lead times • Higher delivery costs	Early-stage companies without a lot of national coverage who need to maximize their cash and minimize complexity
Regional	• Shorter delivery times • Lower delivery costs	• Higher inventory holding costs • Increased complexity	More mature startups (3-5 years) with significant national coverage and a need to reach customers in <5 days from order receipt
Hub and Spoke	• Overnight delivery options and average lead times of 1-2 days • Sophisticated eComm integrations and lots of flexibility managing special eComm requests	• Typically, not as reliable or mature for wholesale businesses • Warehousing and handling costs tend to be higher than more traditional 3PLs • Constraints on bundling multi-SKU orders	eCommerce focused companies (>60% of volume in eComm)

Figure 14. Sample distribution network

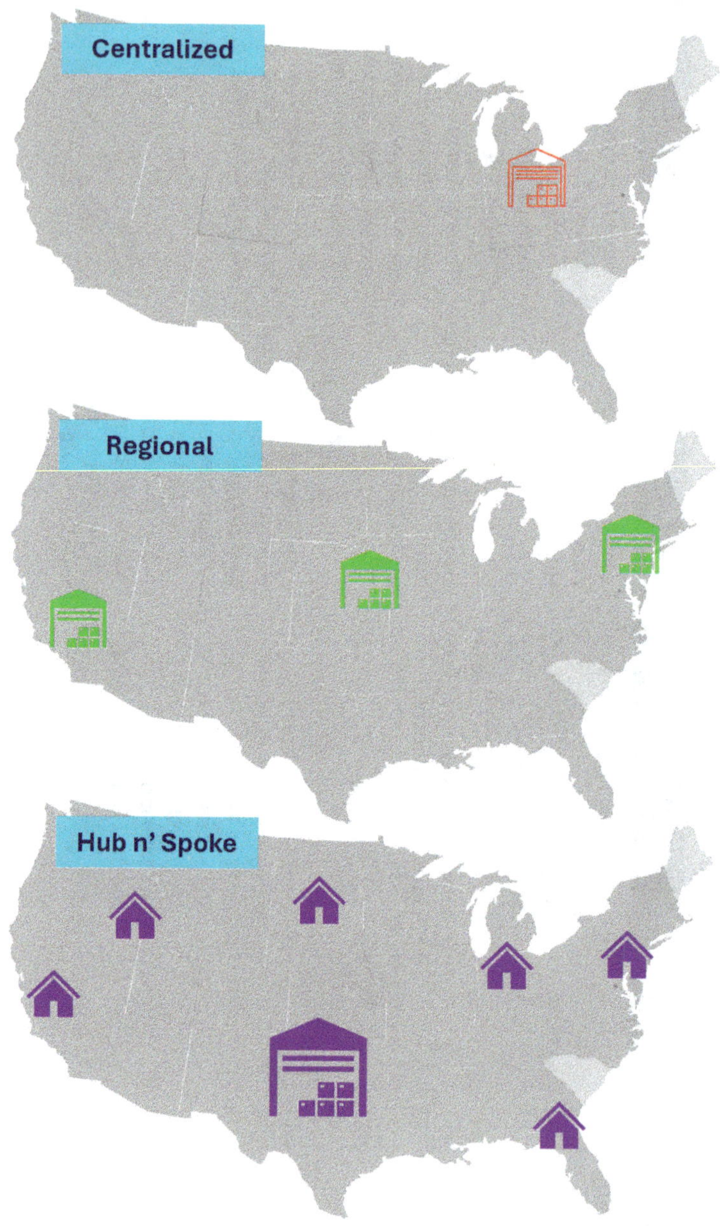

Figure 14, continued. Sample distribution network

WHOLESALE NORMS

After you've designed the network, you will be eager to get the 3PL up and running. However, there are several more critical steps to align before you can cement the relationship. As mentioned above, I like to think about distribution and order fulfillment through the two primary channels: wholesale and ecommerce. Wholesale will eventually command the bulk of the volume for most successful consumer product companies. Depending on your business, the margins in wholesale could be better or worse, based primarily on shipping cost. Often, the ecommerce channel will have higher margins, because you cut out the middleman (i.e. a distributor). But that leads to a fundamental difference, which is A&P (advertising and promotion). Ecommerce requires a much higher A&P spend per unit, which is why you'll ultimately look to sell larger volumes to wholesale (between 70–80% of total volume for a slightly more mature company). Ecommerce is a great place to introduce your brand to the world, but wholesale is where you make your hay. Put simply, would you rather sell two pouches on eComm to 2M different customers or ship 4M pouches to 20–40 concentrated customers at the national level? Wholesale is how you properly scale a business. Therefore, you will want to ensure your 3PL can support your wholesale business efficiently and reliably. Here are a few considerations as you build out your relationship norms.

Relationship Norms

1. ***Working Standards:*** Define a schedule for regular status updates. We used a weekly check-in call. The agenda for that call should address open or late orders, review KPIs,

inventory checks, quality or system issues, and discuss opportunities for future projects.

2. ***SOPs (Standard Operating Procedures):*** Establish norms for all the key processes.
   i. ***Order Management:*** Specify how the orders will be sent from your customers to the 3PL. Early on, you'll likely need to send them through email or some kind of shared spreadsheet. Your 3PL should have its own system and you may be able to enter the orders directly through their portal. Ultimately, you will want to use an EDI (electronic data interface), which is a platform such as SPS commerce. These platforms allow the end customer to submit their orders and have the order directly received by the 3PL.
   ii. ***Order Processing Time:*** Should be ~48 hours (from the time of submission, it should be staged and ready for pickup within 48 hours).
   iii. ***FEFO (First Expired, First Out)/FIFO (First In, First Out):*** This is especially important if you have a shelf life. Specify that the product must be shipped in order of expiration date or when the product was first received.
   iv. ***Physical Inventory Counts:*** How often do they need to count your inventory? This should be at least annual, likely bi-annual, or even quarterly depending on product cost.
   v. ***Shrinkage Factor:*** The contract should specify how much shrinkage the 3PL is allowed. This is the maximum allowable buffer between the system totals and physical counts. Anything exceeding the shrinkage

factor will be charged to the 3PL (product COGS will be reimbursed). This should typically range between 0.05-0.5% max. It should definitely be <1%.

3. ***Standard Costs***: When building the quote, most 3PL's will include some form of the following types of costs:
   i. ***Storage:*** This should be on a per pallet basis. It varies widely depending on where the facility is located and how it is stored. As of 2025, common rates are typically between $10-20 per pallet.
   ii. ***Order Prep:*** There will be a fee to prep orders. These fees should vary depending on whether the order is a full pallet or requires a breakdown of mixed cases. The full pallet orders should obviously be much more economical, since they require little prep work.
   iii. ***Inbound and Outbound Fees:*** There will be charges to receive and ship pallets out the door.
   iv. ***Freight:*** If your 3PL provides last mile transportation or passes through UPS/Fed Ex, you should negotiate prices for standard lanes (i.e. from your co-packer to the 3PL or from the 3PL to standard, large customers in the same locations). A key point on logistics as a whole: ***freight will significantly exceed the cost of storage and order prep, usually by a factor of 3-4x***. So, make some concessions on storage if it will get you a better deal on freight.
4. ***KPI Tracking:*** The 3PL should provide a report or a dashboard to track performance on the key metrics. These should include adherence to all the SOP items listed above.

Inventory Norms and DOH per Warehouse

One of the keys to managing your inventory is to determine the days-on-hand (DOH) inventory to keep in storage at each warehouse. This is the target set to ensure sufficient product in the warehouse to cover the demand plan. Recall we used this concept back in the **Supply Planning** section to determine the size of the production runs. We did this exercise at the aggregate level to cover total demand. Now, we've added the concept of a network of DCs supporting different portions of your overall volume. Thus, we'll need to apply the same logic to adjust inventory levels to the target DOH at the warehouse level. Note that the target DOH remains the same across all warehouses. So, if you determined 40-60 days is the target, that is the target for all warehouse nodes.

Shelf-life plays a huge factor in determining this target. We touched on this briefly, but I'll reiterate. For products with longer shelf-lives, you can keep larger amounts of inventory on-hand. Holding more inventory requires tying up your cash, which is not ideal. However, in the early stages, there will be higher volatility in your demand plan. As discussed several times, going out of stock is a nightmare scenario, so you need to keep a little extra inventory to circumvent that possibility. Once you get a bit more history and confidence in your demand plan, you can ratchet down the DOH to industry standards. If your product has a lower shelf-life like beer, you'll have to reduce these levels significantly. As a general rule, and one that several distributors like KeHE enforce, **you should plan to have at least 75% of the shelf-life remaining when you ship your product to distributors**. For direct customers, that number can be slightly lower (closer to 60-70%).

See the ***DC Inventory Levels*** in the supplemental materials and Figure 15 below.

This exercise works in tandem with Supply Planning. For example, during Supply Planning, we determined a production volume of 1,200 cases of Fruit Punch in Jan-26. We now need to determine how to split those cases between the different DCs. After completing the DOH

Factor	DOH (Days on Hand)
Absolute Min	50
Target Min	70
Target Max	90
Absolute Max	110

Adjustable cell
Calculated cell

Target range
Moderate range
Out of range

DC	Days per month	31	28	31	30	31	30	31	31	30	31	30	31
East	Fruit Punch	Jan-26	Feb-26	Mar-26	Apr-26	May-26	Jun-26	Jul-26	Aug-26	Sep-26	Oct-26	Nov-26	Dec-26
	1. Inventory	400	683	466	549	332	565	348	581	364	547	330	563
	2. Forecast Demand	217	217	217	217	217	217	217	217	217	217	217	217
	3. Open PO (Prod Order)	500	0	300	0	450	0	450	0	400	0	450	0
	4. Ending Inv	683	466	549	332	565	348	581	364	547	330	563	346
	5. Days On-Hand	93	66	77	47	80	49	82	51	77	47	78	48
Central	Fruit Punch	Jan-26	Feb-26	Mar-26	Apr-26	May-26	Jun-26	Jul-26	Aug-26	Sep-26	Oct-26	Nov-26	Dec-26
	1. Inventory	200	303	205	308	210	263	165	343	220	448	275	403
	2. Forecast Demand	98	98	98	98	98	98	123	123	123	173	173	173
	3. Open PO (Prod Order)	200	0	200	0	150	0	300	0	350	0	300	0
	4. Ending Inv	303	205	308	210	263	165	343	220	448	275	403	230
	5. Days On-Hand	92	64	96	61	71	41	75	43	80	50	74	43
West	Fruit Punch	Jan-26	Feb-26	Mar-26	Apr-26	May-26	Jun-26	Jul-26	Aug-26	Sep-26	Oct-26	Nov-26	Dec-26
	1. Inventory	800	999	698	897	596	995	594	943	542	791	490	839
	2. Forecast Demand	301	301	301	301	301	401	401	401	301	301	301	301
	3. Open PO (Prod Order)	500	0	500	0	700	0	750	0	550	0	650	0
	4. Ending Inv	999	698	897	596	995	594	943	542	791	490	839	538
	5. Days On-Hand	98	71	81	50	76	50	86	55	81	50	84	54

Figure 15. Target DOH by Warehouse

exercise at the DC level, you can see I decided to send 500 cases to the East DC, 200 cases to the Central DC, and 500 cases to the West DC (row 3 above). This will require a bit of trial and error but it's one of the most crucial activities in the early stages for a Start-Ops leader. The dichotomy should be obvious: too much product on hand and you run out of shelf-life, forcing write-offs and wasted cash. Not enough product on hand, you face out of stocks and your competitors steal your share. If you misallocate the product across DCs, you end up shuttling product from one DC to another. This destroys any value created by the network DC approach. Optimization is key, starting with these guidelines and tweaking with some trial and error.

ECOMMERCE NORMS

All points in the wholesale section apply to your ecommerce business. There are some additional elements you will need to consider specific to ecommerce, as part of your overall 3PL relationship.

eCommerce Additions

1. ***Order Prep:*** Your co-packer will need to support ecomm order preparation. Typically, you will produce your product in a multi-unit wholesale box at your co-packer. You may need your 3PL to repack these items into a single unit box or a multi-pack box for consumer use. You can ship product directly to Amazon in wholesale format and have them prep the order, depending on the product type. This can be a problem for more premium products. Amazon might grab your high-end product, slap on some bubble wrap, and toss it in a box with baby wipes and spatulas. Not the

best consumer experience! Work with your 3PL to align on rates for standard prep work and ad-hoc kitting.

2. ***Packaging Considerations:*** I suggest printing the Amazon FNSKU (fulfillment network SKU) on each box (see Figure 16 below). This is what Amazon will use to distribute your product through their network. You can also setup your 3PL to use this product-specific identifier to trace the product through their warehouse network. Essentially, your 3PL will have a WMS (warehouse management system) that they will use to coordinate and track inventory movement; they can do this with a UPC (the code on the consumer package) or any other internal SKU code. This is why I recommend using the FNSKU for your 3PL, to make it consistent with Amazon's requirements. They will also accept a UPC, so check out some YouTube videos and decide which one makes the most sense for your product.
3. ***Bundling:*** Another item to consider is how to create consumer bundle packs. When consumers order multiple products, they expect to receive all their products at once. Some brands like to use pre-made bundles to support this activity and encourage higher AOV (average order value). For example, a company might make a ***summer trio kit*** with seasonal products ideal for the summer months. I am a strong supporter of this tactic, but I highly encourage **digital execution over physical bundling** for early-stage startups. The best way to achieve this is to create one SKU-specific box for each product. Then, place listings on your website and Amazon for the bundle pack (i.e. the summer trio). Finally, you link the underlying products to this kit, so when someone orders the summer trio kit, the system automatically pulls one of each product in that

bundle. It receives the order as if three separate products were ordered under the base SKUs. The benefit of this approach is simplicity. The alternative would be to create summer trio specific boxes. Now you added a new box, to which you need to negotiate a price, develop the material, manage the inventory, etc. Now do this for every combination of bundle products! It spirals very quickly and becomes limiting on what offerings you can post. When you set it up as digital bundles, you can have as many bundles as you want and the execution in supply is exactly the same as standard orders. A small tradeoff for the consumer is a huge windfall of simplification for the Ops team.

Figure 16. eComm Box with FNSKU

Expansion On eComm Network Design

We covered the network design with the centralized, regional, and hub and spoke models. Depending on which model you select, eCommerce will be impacted. Below are 3 options for eCommerce management:

1. ***Hybrid Fulfillment:*** In this model, you equip your 3PL to fulfill website orders and activate Amazon's ***Fulfillment by***

Amazon (FBA) for Amazon orders. Typically, your 3PL can reduce freight costs versus the alternative options by bundling the product in a single box. Amazon FBA usually manages your Amazon orders without many problems and using FBA enables the *Prime* badge. Also, you can configure this model to provide contingencies if you run into out of stocks (i.e. if Amazon is out of stock, your 3PL can fill the Amazon orders using Fulfillment by Merchant (FBM). This model leads to the highest service rate and typically the lowest costs.

2. *MCF Through Amazon:* You can send all your products to Amazon and have them manage fulfillment of both Amazon and website orders. This isn't necessarily a bad option in the early stages. It provides a lot of simplification. Dump all your product in one location, aggregate total eComm sales by SKU for forecasting, and you're off and running. The two big challenges here are service and cost. Amazon is a giant company and, in the beginning, you likely won't have a dedicated customer rep. If you run into problems getting inventory checked into their system, you could be out of stock for prolonged periods of time. Additionally, the last mile freight cost is usually about 15-20% higher on a per unit basis.
3. *FBM Across All Channels:* The second alternative is to fulfill all your orders from your 3PL, including Amazon orders. The issue with this approach is that you will lose the Prime badge, which lowers sales (typically around 15-20%). The potential reduced costs are offset by the lost revenue. I just wanted to mention it, so you were aware of the options.

ORDER MANAGEMENT

The last point to discuss in logistics is order management. You will need to develop a system for receiving inbound orders, transmitting those orders to the 3PL for fulfillment, and tracking the completion of those orders. This is pretty basic and will depend on the technical sophistication of your 3PL's WMS. I'll give you a few highlights:

Order Management Best Practices

1. *eComm Integration:* You will want to setup an integration with your ecommerce orders. Ensure your 3PL can integrate with your website hosting platform (i.e. Shopify) and Amazon seller central. You will also want to ensure that your ERP system is integrated with both these platforms to register sales and deplete inventory. Depending on product category, sales will be in the hundreds and eventually thousands of units per day. Processing, fulfilling, and accounting for these orders can only scale with back-end integrations.
2. *Transfer Log*: This is the standard point when I caveat that, ideally, the orders will be fully integrated. However, early on, you need to use some shared sheets. We created a simple Excel sheet for internal purposes called the transfer log to track transfers of materials with the 3PL. It had 3 basic tabs:
    i. *Inbound FGs:* After production at the co-packer, you will need to transfer goods, both physically and systematically, to the respective 3PL warehouse. While you can see individual transfers through your ERP reporting, it was helpful to have a repository of transfers for planning and tracking purposes (see Figure 17).

ii. *eComm conversion*: The 3PL will be converting products into ecommerce-ready packaging and shipping out product to Amazon. We created a log to house the forecast and track the progress of each eComm bulk order. **Note: This is not the individual consumer orders.** As I mentioned, those will all come through via integration. This is the bulk prep and shipments to Amazon or pre-prep work for your website orders. For example, we might have the 3PL prep 5,000 bottles of Fruit Punch and ship those to Amazon. I also might have them prep 3,000 bottles of Fruit Punch to keep in house at the 3PL, in anticipation of the next 6-8 weeks of website sales via Shopify. The transfer log was used to forecast those bulk conversions and track the progress of completing the orders (see Figure 18).

iii. *Wholesale Shipments:* Lastly, you'll want to keep a list of all the outbound wholesale orders you have received. This information is also available in your ERP system reports, but we found value in tracking the in-progress nature of the orders via the sheet. It also helped with internal, cross-functional coordination, as many folks on the team will need to know what orders are coming, but might not have the time to pull a bunch of reports (i.e. the field sales team). Below is a snapshot of how we used this document (see Figure 19).

Note that each of these items will be formally transmitted to the 3PL. Ideally, this will happen in their WMS. The transfer log should be used for internal purposes. If the 3PL isn't technically sophisticated, it can be used to transmit orders. However, if the 3PL doesn't have the ability to receive orders via EDI (electronic data interface) or some type of automated/semi-automated system, you probably need to vet a few more 3PL options.

5-C. The Wrap: Quick Facts for Benchmarks

The distribution network was an area I deferred for several years, and it became a constant battle. One the axioms that drives me nuts is, "If it ain't broke, don't fix it." I don't know where that phrase originated but if I had to guess, it's probably from someone with a toolbox sporting a bumper sticker that reads ***"Local ####."*** The problem here is that most of the time, there's really no such distinction as "broke" or "not broke". There are degrees of broken and degrees of working. If you aren't constantly optimizing, you're losing in relation to your competition. Whenever the question of why American manufacturing declined so much over the last 50 years arises, the reflexive response is usually something to do with wages. "We can't compete with low-wage labor in third world countries." While labor cost is a factor, America had the highest wages in the world in the 1950's, by a much larger ratio than today. And yet, America was the preeminent manufacturer in the world back then, producing ~70% of world's total automobiles.

The gap between American wages and Chinese wages is much lower today than it was in the '50's, yet China has usurped the U.S. as the leading manufacturing country. This was largely achieved through capital investment, innovation, and continuous improvement (and obviously by opening up Capitalist markets). The most important metric is landed cost per unit, which is driven by the **total output over a whole series of costs** (including labor but also logistics, raw

FG Item	Total Qty Produced
FG-16z Fruit Punch 12pk	1150
FG-16z Grape 12pk	970
FG-16z Pimento Punch 12pk	145

FG Item	Item Code	Qty to transfer	DC
FG-16z Fruit Punch 12pk	10001	345	East
FG-16z Fruit Punch 12pk	10001	230	Central
FG-16z Fruit Punch 12pk	10001	575	West
FG-16z Grape 12pk	10002	291	East
FG-16z Grape 12pk	10002	194	Central
FG-16z Grape 12pk	10002	485	West
FG-16z Pimento Punch 12pk	10003	44	East
FG-16z Pimento Punch 12pk	10003	29	Central
FG-16z Pimento Punch 12pk	10003	73	West

Figure 17. Inbound Transfer of FGs to DCs

Date	Flavor	SKU	Bottles	Cases (items/case)	Cases/Pallet	Pallets	Shipment Plan Created?	Physical Status	ERP Status	ERP Transfer #	Origin	Destination
1/6/2026	Fruit Punch	X002XEWR8P	4,800	400	100	4	Complete	Complete	Open		Central	Amazon
1/6/2026	Grape	X002MKLR7Y	3,600	300	100	3	Complete	Complete	Open		Central	Amazon
1/6/2026	Pimento Punch	X002LOPE2C	1,200	100	100	1	Complete	Complete	Open		Central	Amazon
1/20/2026	Fruit Punch	X002XEWR8P	4,800	400	100	4	Open	Open	Open		Central	Central for Website sales
1/20/2026	Grape	X002MKLR7Y	3,600	300	100	3	Open	Open	Open		Central	Central for Website sales
1/20/2026	Pimento Punch	X002LOPE2C	1,200	100	100	1	Open	Open	Open		Central	Central for Website sales

Figure 18. eComm Kitting Forecast and Transfers

Order Received Date	Requested / Planned Ship Date	FG Item	Item Code	Case Qty	Customer	Physical Status	Invoice Sent	Origin	Customer PO #
1/6/2026	1/16/2026	FG-16z Fruit Punch 12pk	10001	100	Wal-Mart	Complete	Complete	Central	34545
1/6/2026	1/16/2026	FG-16z Grape 12pk	10002	50	Wal-Mart	Complete	Complete	Central	34545
1/6/2026	1/16/2026	FG-16z Pimento Punch 12pk	10003	30	Wal-Mart	Complete	Open	Central	34545
1/8/2026	1/22/2026	FG-16z Fruit Punch 12pk	10001	200	7-Eleven	Complete	Open	West	P4231
1/8/2026	1/22/2026	FG-16z Grape 12pk	10002	200	7-Eleven	Complete	Open	West	P4231
1/10/2026	1/23/2026	FG-16z Pimento Punch 12pk	10003	50	Ahmed's Grocery	Open	Open	West	A8795

Figure 19. Wholesale Shipments to Customers

and packaging materials, and a slew of overhead costs). Chinese manufacturers have focused on continuous improvement, while American manufacturers have allowed complacency to eliminate our former advantages. A Start-Ops leader should have a similar mindset of continuous improvement and ditch age-old adages that don't apply. Complacency is the enemy of the Start-Ops leader.

I've already mentioned my aversion to inventory management. The bulk of those problems were experienced before I built a robust, 3PL-driven network. It will likely be a bit more upfront cost than storing your product at the co-packer, but these incremental costs usually pay back on the first physical inventory count. It also enables better results in one of the startup company's most important metrics: case fill rate. By getting closer to the customer, it will facilitate shorter lead times for delivery. This is going to be a huge factor when big orders arrive at the last minute. I view the Sales team as the key customer of the Ops function. If you need to tell your customer you can't fill an order, you haven't done your job as the Start-Ops leader. The 3PL network is like stretching after a difficult workout; you've done everything right to that moment but if you skip the final step, you lose a lot of those potential gains. Here are a few benchmarks on the distribution model:

Factor	Benchmark
Cost as % of Revenue	5-15% is considered a pretty standard range. The lighter weight products should obviously be on the low end of this range.
Pallet storage	As of 2025, the monthly cost should be between $10–20 to store pallets.
Pallet intake fees	Should be similar to storage fees, sometimes a bit higher ($15–20 per pallet).

Factor	Benchmark
Pallet turns	Products with longer shelf-lives (>1 year) should turn a minimum of 4–6 times per year, meaning you should not be holding these pallets at your 3PL for more than 2-3 months.
Rule of thumb on remaining inventory	Shipping to a distributor: ensure at least 75% of your total shelf-life is still remaining. Shipping direct to a customer: at least 60% remaining.
Inventory accuracy	The physical inventory counts should yield at least 99.5% accuracy. Established companies will contract higher rates (99.9% accuracy).
Case fill rate (CFR)	Startup companies need very high CFR (97-99%).
SOP for order turnaround	The 3PL should be able to turnaround an order from the date the order is dropped to out the door in 72 hours.
Delivery lead times to customer	You should be able to reach every customer in no more than 5 days (eComm possibly a bit lower, closer to 3 days).

PILLAR 6

NEW PRODUCT DEVELOPMENT

6-A. The Situation: Setting the Scene

We've reached the final stage in this journey, and I left the most exciting part for last. I think a strong case could be made that breakthrough innovation—the development of novel products and nascent categories that change the way people live—is the backbone of the modern American economy. Being part of the progression from ideation through development and into commercialization is a type of career fulfillment one can only experience in entrepreneurship. True, large companies do innovation, but usually they follow trends and hedge risks, rather than do anything truly revolutionary (which is why big companies tend to not do innovation very well).

As I was preparing to write this section, I contemplated some of the differences between life at a startup company versus large companies or the public sector. It made me think of this old Milton Friedman story. He was visiting the Soviet Union in 1970's to get a sense of how a centrally-planned economy worked. He went to a job site and noticed a bunch of men digging a ditch. He asked the supervisor, "Why aren't they using a bulldozer?" The foreman replied "Oh, this is a jobs program. We use shovels to maximize the number of men on the job." Freidman quipped, "Well in that case, why don't you give them spoons!" This silly example is at the core of what makes entrepreneurship and new product development so special. All the incentives are aligned to avoid decisions that make no sense. If you do something stupid, you will be punished. If you do something smart, you will be rewarded. The market is the ultimate arbiter of truth. There are a ton of these perverse incentives in the public sector, but they also exist in the private sector at large firms. I referenced these earlier as ***diseconomies of scale***. When each manager is responsible for his or her own P&L, decisions are made which aren't in the best interest of the parent company. This happens every day in big CPG.

This is the beauty of new product development. At the end of the day, you need to create products that people want to buy, at a financially viable cost, and build a plan to route these products to market. Simple as this sounds, it's the hardest thing to do in business. Liberation comes from the fact that results are completely objective in terms of success or failure. You will know months after launch if you've created a timeless classic or another waste management special.

In the same way that Dave Chappelle can't teach someone to write jokes like him, I can't teach you how to create breakthrough innovation. That's not what this chapter is about. This chapter is to provide a framework conducive to the creation of successful new products. I am not a visionary creator in the way the founders of Ritual are and that's okay. My role was always to harness their vision and guide the development. It was to manifest the great ideas into reality and shelve the dogs before they became waste management specials. This is what we will cover in the following section.

6-B. The Core: Section Contents

- Objective: How to conduct the new product development process and evaluate the results
- Key Components:
    - Inonovation Basics
    - Portfolio Assessment
    - Resources
    - Commercialization Management
    - Introduction of New Products
    - Testing and Validation

INNOVATION BASICS

Since pillar 1, we've worked under the assumption that you already have your product in place. To do so likely required one of two possible routes: you launched a new product with different features in an existing category or you created a new category altogether. A good example of the former is Chomps. Beef sticks had existed for decades, but they were loaded with sugar and preservatives, which Chomps looked to rectify. Ritual is a good example of the latter. As you might expect, the two scenarios come with different challenges. In the Chomps scenario, it's much easier to explain the proposition to already educated consumers. They know what beef sticks are and they are aware of the problems with sugar and preservatives. The bigger challenge is taking market share from very established, well-capitalized competition.

In the Ritual case, it's blue skies as far as the eye can see, but you need to get the sails out. There is virtually no competition at the start, but the challenge is explaining why your product should exist. We spent the majority of the first year explaining why anyone would want a margarita without alcohol. Quick side note: our marketing team approached this challenge by building a loyal army of insider influencers. We elevated their online voices to the point where they started doing the advocating and educating on our behalf, which enabled us to focus on selling. This is an effective, organic technique. Back to the task at hand. I wanted to lay out these two routes so you could get a sense of the product development challenges. In the existing category, winning shelf-space is the primary retail challenge. In the new category, you need to convince a retailer to create the shelf-space. Both scenarios land on the same conclusion: don't launch too many SKUs. I recommend launching **two or three SKUs maximum to start**.

Let's fast-forward in the process. You launched your two (or three) SKUs. It was a huge success, which is any scenario in which you aren't out of business after 12 months. At this point, it's a good idea to establish a new product development (NPD) meeting, led by operations. Ritual had a highly creative management team, and tons of ideas were flowing around the office every day in year one. Many of the ideas were not commercially viable and would have been incredibly detrimental to our growth by distracting us from our core mission. Some of these ideas were highly incremental and would further establish our hold on the burgeoning category we helped create. What we really needed was a formal funnel of ideas, a methodology for rating and validating the viability of these ideas, and a process for driving them through commercialization and into the marketplace. That might sound a little corporate. It might sound like something that would stifle creativity. This is the opposite of the truth. Although counter-intuitive, there are myriad studies demonstrating that adding some constraints improves creativity. If I give someone a blank sheet of paper and say, "Write me something funny," that's a pretty challenging task. Give someone the same blank sheet of paper but add, "You have two business consultants in a room interviewing an underperforming employee," and you might come back with "What would you say you do here"?

Innovation works similarly. When the first products were created, it was the blank sheet of paper exercise. However, now the constraints exist. It's the job of the Ops team to reinforce the necessary constraints, while eliminating the superfluous ones. This is another area where big companies struggle. They concoct too many constraints and squash the innovative nature of the products. You need to thread the needle, and that requires thinking with the right combination of structure and creativity. As Jordan Peterson would call it, you need to find the balance between chaos and order. The first step is to establish these meetings and conduct a portfolio assessment.

PORTFOLIO ASSESSMENT

The first NPD meeting should be a longer session with lots of pre-work. The goal of the session is to evaluate your current portfolio of products, ensure all the current products should remain active, identify products missing from your roster, consider alternative formats, and wrap up on what's needed. Hopefully, your team is expanding at this stage in the game, and you have finance support. The end of year one was when we brought in a dedicated finance lead that allowed me to focus on operations (and firmly established that I never wanted to do finance again). Grab this person and the most analytical resource from the marketing and/or sales functions. Quick side note: Ritual hired a dedicated ecommerce lead near the end of our first year. He was an expert on Amazon seller central, Shopify, and the deployment and optimization of marketing funds. He was a vital part of our early success, which was largely driven by ecomm. If you can work this into the budget, this resource pays for itself very quickly by improving your ROAS and average order value. Gather up the dream team, which should be 3-4 people, and start with the assessment pre-work. You'll need to pull the following data:

Portfolio Assessment Data

1. ***Competition***: Build a list of all your competitors.
2. ***Products:*** Expand that list into the specific product SKUs.
3. ***Volume and Growth:*** Estimate how much volume each brand and product sold in the last 12 months. Ideally, compare that to the previous 12 months. This is an easier exercise to conduct with the established categories, with the use of Nielsen data. In nascent categories, pull Amazon and Shopify data through some of their add-on services. You may need to use press on the category. You can try to get some details directly from retailers. It's a difficult exercise but doesn't need to be precise. You should be able to get a good idea of who's winning and losing in the current landscape.
4. ***Price:*** Layer in the product price.
5. ***Format:*** Separate this assessment by product format (i.e. 750mL glass bottles vs. 12 oz cans in the ready-to-drink (RTD) format).
6. ***Customer Ratings:*** Grab these from Amazon, Google, and even product competitions. There is a slew of CPG competitions where products are rated and awarded various statuses. The San Francisco Wine and Spirits rated our Aperitif as a double gold, which means every judge rated

it as a gold (chalk that up as an innovation success). That info is readily available to our competitors.

7. ***Total Score:*** Weigh these KPIs and assign a total score to rank order the field.

This probably sounds like a shockingly obvious exercise. I posit that very few companies thoroughly conduct it as I just laid out. While the benefits of the process are obvious, it's a lot of work and requires discipline and creativity to assemble. If you've ever seen one of those companies that launches 15 new products in a couple of years, the vast majority of which compete with themselves, I can assure you they didn't do this exercise. Cannibalization of your existing products with new products is a serious problem for startups with limited capital. Spend the time upfront on this portfolio assessment. It's an investment that will pay back in spades.

After assembling your grid of the current landscape, it's time to conduct the group meeting. Review the current landscape and identify high-ranked products that you don't currently produce. Determine if it makes sense to expand into similar/adjacent SKUs. Additionally, review your formats and determine if it's time to extend into new sizes or package types. Lastly, do some brainstorming on what still doesn't exist but should. This is the piece that can really drive some innovative ideas. Again, having reviewed everything out there illuminates what ***isn't*** out there, but really should be.

After completing this exercise, you should have a map of areas to exploit. However, it's crucial not to pursue all these ideas at once. Reconvene the portfolio team in a couple weeks, after you've had time to build the timelines and work with finance on the size of the prize. Finally, create a roadmap of launch plans for these different products over the next three years. Balance the mix between the easiest to launch and the biggest ideas. A good way to approach this is to launch a line extension first, which is a new variant in the same packaging format. Then, add the bigger innovation project on an 18–24-month horizon. This enables a good mix of new offerings to the market, while providing sufficient time to conduct truly breakthrough innovation. On that note, we'll now discuss the typical timelines for various project types.

STANDARD TIMELINES

Building the roadmap of products requires an understanding of the basic workstreams and standard lead times of each product type. I'm going to provide the startup version of these timelines. Big CPG companies will spend 25-40% more time on each of these projects. They do this to reduce liability and protect the reputation of their full product portfolio. You have an advantage in this capacity since you don't have any other brands. However, back to the quality section, a PR-screw up probably means you're out of business. So, weigh the good with the bad. Below are the different project types and associated lead-times:

Project Categories

1. ***Renovation – 6 months***: This includes graphics changes, new boxes, new labels, etc—product touch-ups that don't require new parts in manufacturing. Marketing teams can get "renovation-happy" and want to make these updates very frequently. In my experience, they usually drive little incremental sales. This will be some of the creative tension between Marketing and Ops. Make sure you keep them in check on these updates and can demonstrate the need for

the changes. Also, make it clear that once we change this item, it will stay that way for the foreseeable future.

2. ***Line Extension – 9 months***: This is a new flavor in the same packaging format. These items drive the most bang for the buck in the early stages. If you already have a retailer with three SKUs, they will often bring in the fourth SKU right away (a 33% lift in average items carried (AIC)). That is under the assumption that you've done the portfolio assessment and launched something truly incremental.
3. ***New Format – 12 months***: This involves putting existing product in a different packaging container. Smaller formats can drive incremental placements and faster rates of sale. They can also be highly cannibalistic and margin dilutive, so proceed with caution. Ensure you price these products at a premium on a per volume basis. This is like the time Kramer bought the industrial sized cans of Beef-a-reeno at the price club in ***Seinfeld***. Discount the larger formats and put the small formats at a price premium.
4. ***New to World – 18-24 months***: This is the output of the missing items brainstorm in the portfolio assessment. If you've established a brand, it's possible to extend it into a new category. These are major investments and will typically require additional capital expenditure (like plant equipment or packaging molds). First, ensure your team has the bandwidth to drive the base business on top of this initiative. Otherwise, you may need to add some resources to focus exclusively on the new to world. Second, ensure the investors know your plans. Be upfront with them as you pivot to this new category.

Overlay these timelines onto the projects generated in the portfolio assessment and you've got your pipeline. Each project comes with a detailed timeline of workstreams. I'll probably expand on those in the *Start-Ops Playbook* YouTube channel I previously mentioned. You can do some basic research on the nuts and bolts of each project and get a clearer picture. Conduct the NPD meeting on a weekly or bi-weekly basis to drive these projects. I would add that this task is one of the more annoying responsibilities of a Start-Ops leader. You think "facilitating meetings, updating timelines, sending out notes; isn't this why I left corporate America for startup life?" While all of that is true, it is such a crucial component of the organization as whole, it's going to require an operational drumbeat. I've seen too many companies with very promising products fizzle out in a couple of years because they botched the innovation function. They launched too many stupid products, too quickly, with no plan for how these items would co-exist or how they would support them in retail. In short, suck it up and help provide the order to accompany the chaos.

INTRODUCING THE NEW PRODUCTS

"A great product sells itself" is not actually true. There are several considerations to keep in mind when introducing these products to the market. First, map out the route to market. We discussed this in previous sections, but it might be a little different in new product launches. Is there a particular retail environment conducive to announcing this product to the world? This matters because sales channels have different shelf reset windows and you will want to align your product launch accordingly. Generally speaking, large national retailers like Walmart, Target, and Kroger have fixed reset windows, 2-4 times per year. If you are making a seasonal product, best suited for summer, you need to align the commercialization timeline for a spring reset. The regional retailers tend to have more flexibility in this capacity. You might be able to make a big splash by offering an exclusive launch to one regional chain. This can help to ensure focus on execution and provide tangible evidence of the product viability. After three months of selling like gang busters, you can take these data to the national chains and show proof of concept. The key point here is to connect your product strategy to the retailer's operating calendar, rather than work in a vacuum.

Next, consider how you will support consumer education in market. The retailer will be excited to see innovation from you, but they will be cautious of how much investment to make in educating your prospective consumers. Show them you have a plan for in-store and out-of-store education, across omni-channels. When you demo the product, it's helpful to also show the point-of-sale merchandise to accompany it on shelf.

Lastly, think about risk on both sides of the spectrum. It is true that introducing a risky product can cripple your brand, tarnish your reputation, and put you out of business. Be cognizant of that and make sure the products you introduce fit your brand guidelines. The portfolio assessment should help flesh that out. However, it's also risky to introduce products that are too conservative and don't disrupt the current offerings.

Let me give you an example of this from my past in big CPG. I worked on a cross-branded product for the Kraft Foods Group. Kraft was battling to stay relevant with consumers actively looking for healthy, fresh, less processed food. There was a big protein craze at the time and Kraft was well-positioned to pounce with Planters nuts, Oscar Mayer, and cheese in its portfolio. We developed a concept called P3, intended to contain three types of protein in a single tray: meat, cheese, and nuts. It was a really promising idea with substantial market opportunities. We began the naming processes and landed what seemed like a slam dunk: The Protein Power Pack (P3). Concepts were developed in accordance with this positioning, including a tray shaped like a dumbbell, to reinforce the idea of power.

In the eleventh hour, the legal team stepped in and squashed the name. The rationale had something to do with the product not "technically" providing "power" to the consumer and our inability to substantiate that claim in a consumer study. We settled on Portable Protein Pack. The dumbbell tray now made no sense, and the product no longer spoke to the consumer target. Overall, the product was still a decent success, largely due to its functionality. I can't prove it, but I feel the product would have been more successful if launched as it was intended to be. The point here is to illustrate the potential downside of neutering the soul of your product for risk avoidance. It is much easier for a company like Kraft to introduce a new product than a couple of startup entrepreneurs, since they already have the retail footprint. If you believe in a concept, you need to take a little risk and make it stand out on a crowded shelf. The Airbnb guys didn't ask for permission. They built a loyal army of consumers who loved their product offering so much, no legislator could squash their business. Stick to your guns and drive your vision to the market.

TESTING AND VALIDATION

I've tried to make most of this playbook fact-based and avoid sweeping assertions. Having said that, we're going to slightly diverge from that approach in this section. Much like the binarization of our society politically, there tends to be a sizable divide on data vs. intuition, where both sides argue that the other side is clueless. The reality to me is somewhere in between. You can and should use data as a guide to better understand where and how to place the guardrails around your idea generation. However, in the end, I believe you need to have a special kind of intuition to properly project successful innovation vs. waste management specials. I love the quote by one of my favorite economists,

Ludwig von Mises, on entrepreneurship: "What distinguishes the successful entrepreneur and promoter from other people is precisely the fact that he does not let himself be guided by what was and is, but arranges his affairs on the ground of his opinion about the future. He sees the past and the present as other people do; but he judges the future in a different way." I think Mises nailed it, and even though this quote is about 100 years old, it's as accurate today as it was then.

This is why I don't have a tremendous amount of confidence in these firms who try to predict the success of your products. It reminds me of "Crisis PR firms," which tend to be as tone deaf as the clients whose careers they are attempting to resuscitate. I feel that, if these people were so good at predicting the future, they would launch their own products instead of testing everyone else's!

I look at data in two distinct groups: authentic and synthetic. Authentic data is crucial to conducting a successful entrepreneurial venture—things like costs, volumes, growth, rate of sale, points of distribution, and many more. To quote the Ritual co-founder Marcus Sakey, (a significantly better author than yours truly), "Nielsen scan data is an unimpeachable source of truth." That's exactly right. This is at the root of the presumption that "people vote with their feet." Speculating on what could be going on when authentic data are available is one of my ultimate pet peeves. I can't stand when people postulate a theory when there are real data right around the corner that simply need to be analyzed. However, this does not apply with synthetic data. These are data sets contrived through simulations, which frequently cannot reliably predict how people will act in the future.

My general advice is to save the money you would spend on these innovation analysis labs. Analyze the market data from your portfolio assessment and lean on your founders to make the call on what to launch and what to shelve.

6-C. The Wrap: Quick Facts for Benchmarks

Warren Buffet has a quote that I've always loved: "When a manager with a sterling reputation takes on a business with a reputation of having shit economics, it's the business's reputation that remains intact" (I'm paraphrasing, but you get the idea). Now replace the word "economics" with "products" and you've got the reality of a startup company. If the products don't taste good, look good, increase performance, improve nutrition, give energy, or in general, improve people's lives, then you have little more on your hands than a "Open for work" LinkedIn badge in escrow. A robust portfolio assessment and rigorous innovation process is going to provide your startup with the best opportunity to launch successful innovation. Here are a few benchmarks:

Factor	Benchmark
Standard lead times	• Renovation: 6 months • Line extension: 9 months • New format: 12 months • New to world: 18-24 months
Recommended SKUs to start the company	2-3
Cost to launch a new product	We didn't discuss the direct costs in line but there are a lot of labor, material, and development fees. Rough estimates are below to give you sense of the hard investment in these initiatives: • Line extension: $200-300K • New format: $400-500K • New to world: $800K-1.2M
NPD Meeting frequency	Conduct these bi-weekly. It's enough to ensure the team stays diligent on their follow-ups, but won't distract from the core business.

IN CLOSING

Ladies and gentlemen, that's a wrap. Five years of exploration, trial and error, victory and defeat, distilled down into the six preceding lessons. I mentioned earlier that we might jump around a bit because it is impossible to align everything in a perfectly sequential order. I'll add that while some of these activities need to be done in parallel, you can't do it all simultaneously. Don't feel like you need to implement every section on day one; that's a recipe for disaster. Set priorities based on your company's trajectory and lifecycle. I say that with the caveat that quality better be somewhere at the top of the list.

I'll leave you with three points to consider, which were previously discussed, but not covered in detail:

1. Integrity: We talked about your responsibility as a Start-Ops leader in the quality section. As you start this new company, anchor your organization's values in operating with integrity. Big companies hold these trainings and instruct their employees to do the right thing, disclose information, avoid conflicts of interest, etc. For most employees, coloring inside the lines at a fortune 500 company is pretty straightforward. At a startup, the lines can get a bit more blurred. You will be the one making these tough decisions,

establishing the standards, negotiating the contracts, and so forth. It becomes very easy to convince yourself that the product you are bringing to market is so important that nobody cares about a couple antiquated standards that probably won't matter much in the long run. I would direct you to a quote from Aldous Huxley: "As if the ends could justify the means. The reality is the **means determine the ends**". If you cut corners and put your customers, your partners, and your employees at risk, you're really putting your company and yourself at risk in the process. When I think of true leadership, I think of the people who focus on the most important issues when they matter the most. It's noteworthy that these almost always correspond with the most difficult things to say in the most difficult moments. Hold true to your core principles, no matter how difficult it is to do so or how easy it is to stray.

2. **Learning**: For the record, five years ago, I had never held a formal position in planning, procurement, quality, or logistics (66% of the playbook)! We could certainly debate whether I know what I'm talking about in these topics, but I hope you can see the learning opportunity afforded to you by the startup experience. Every single day, you learn something new at a startup company, or else it won't be around too long. Soak that up and make the most of it. Capture notes on some of these learnings, which is how I started writing this playbook in the first place. As we discussed, the odds are against your company becoming a long-term success, but I suspect the odds of personal success are in your favor in the long run. Even if the company fails, you have a great opportunity to succeed when the smoke clears.

Carry yourself with humility throughout the process, learn from your mistakes, build long-lasting relationships, and be ready to ascend to new career heights.

3. **Resiliency**: There are days in the startup life of extreme highs, but there are also periods of very dark lows. It seemed like every time one thing went wrong, two or three other issues would quickly follow. This would happen over the course of a couple of days. These aren't minor inconveniences like our product failing a line trial and needing to repeat it. These are issues like inventory shortages when a critical order is due, delays in packaging materials that threaten to cancel production runs, or not being certain how you are going to make payroll. As the Start-Ops leader, you need to weather the storm. It makes me think of that movie ***Any Given Sunday***. For those who remember it, that movie really sucked. It was bad for 95% of the film, lacking credibility, authenticity, and compelling character development. It continued like this all the way up until the very end, when Al Pacino delivered a locker room motivational speech for the ages. I still think it's one of the best monologues I've ever seen. His character dug down deep and put it on the table for everyone to see and rally around. So even though the film was dog shit, that brilliant scene is all I remember. It's the same way at a company in a turbulent pattern, when it feels like nothing can go right. Get your mind focused on doing one thing exactly right that day. Pull out your playbook, take your time, and do it exactly as you always aspired to do, but compromised due to a lack of time, or resources, or whatever excuse you want to use. I found that doing one thing right can turn

> the momentum and you can start chopping away at the mess in front of you. Facing adversity at a startup isn't just a possibility—it's guaranteed. Prepare yourself mentally and stick to your playbook.

I'll leave it to you to take it from here. Keep me posted on how everything is going. I love to hear stories from your start-op experience. Best of luck and savor the process.

APPENDIX A

ACRONYMS & ABBREVIATIONS

3PL – Third party logistics. This is your distribution partner.

ABQ – Always Be Quoting. Procurement survival rule: if you're not comparing bids, you're falling behind.

A&P – Advertising and Promotion. The spend-money to make-money part of your budget.

APC – Aerobic Plate Count. Lab test for micro-organisms. High counts = bad news for your product (and your customers).

BOM – Bill of Materials. Recipe-to-reality guide that turns "batch" into "how many caps, labels, and bottles you actually need."

COA – Certificate of Analysis. The supplier's official certification paperwork for goods receipt.

COGS – Cost of Goods Sold. The true costs to produce and distribute your product.

DC – Distribution Center. A storage warehouse.

DOH – Days on Hand. How many days before the inventory is sold out.

EDI – Electronic Data Interface. The system that lets warehouses talk to each other, so you don't have to send spreadsheets at 2 a.m. Customers submit orders through this portal to your 3PL.

ERP – Enterprise Resource Planning. The all-in-one software that keeps you from drowning in Excel tabs.

FC – Fulfillment Center. These are concentrated facilities, typically used for ecommerce shipments. Amazon uses FCs to store and ship your products.

FGs – Finished Goods. The endgame: finished product ready to sell, ship, and reach your customers.

G&A – General and Administrative. Overhead. The stuff that keeps the lights on.

MRP – Material Resource Plan. The planning tool to calculate material needs for upcoming production runs.

P&L – Profit & Loss Statement. The scoreboard to keep you in the green and in the game.

PAL – Process Authority Letter. A third-party letter, validating the efficacy of your process to produce safe, quality products and provide direction to the contract manufacturer.

PO – Purchase Order. The official form you send to suppliers to complete your material purchases.

RFP – Request for Proposal. Your chance to make suppliers compete for business. A standardized template that allows your suppliers to submit formal bids across a range of criteria.

ROS – Rate of Sale. How fast your product actually moves off shelves, typically measured in sales per day, week, or month.

SO – Sales Order. Record of the specific products, quantities, and prices for goods sold to a customer.

SOP – Standard Operating Procedure. The fundamental processes outlined in your operating manuals.

SWAGU – Scientific Wild-Ass Guess. Rough forecasting that's usually one tweak away from nonsense, but it gets you started in the early days.

WMS – Warehouse Management System. The 3PL's system to manage inventory, receive orders, and track shipments.

ABOUT THE AUTHOR

David DiLoreto completed his MBA from the University of Chicago, Booth School of Business. He is the Chief Operating Officer for Ritual Zero Proof, the nation's leading spirit alternative brand, acquired by Diageo in 2024.

He has over 20 years of experience in operations with consumer brands, from fortune 500's to scrappy startups. The Start-Ops Playbook is a synthesis of these two decades of experience, leveraging the best-in-class tools of the industry benchmarks, through the lens of a startup operator. The goal is to give your company the tools you need to operate like the pros and scrap the ones that get in the way. This enables your startup to move fast and focus on growth, with confidence in the quality and reliability of your supply chain.

Caveats like "having said that…", really drive me nuts. Per Larry David, you say what you really mean, then you reverse it. Having said that, I had to make a lot of caveats in this book! All startups really are different and while the framework remains the same, the targets, thresholds, and decision criteria all come with nuance. I would love to hear more about your startup and the specific challenges you're facing. Connect with me on any of these platforms and check out my YouTube videos for deeper dives. You can use the calendar on my website to book one-on-one sessions.

Website and Social Media

Website:

www.startopsplaybook.com

Supplemental Materials:

www.startopsplaybook.com/resources

YouTube:

www.youtube.com/@start_ops_playbook

Instagram:

@start_ops_playbook

Reddit:

@start_ops_playbook

www.ingramcontent.com/pod-product-compliance
Lightning Source LLC
Chambersburg PA
CBHW071423210326
41597CB00020B/3629

* 9 7 9 8 9 9 3 6 9 1 5 0 3 *